ROMAN LONDON
RECENT ARCHAEOLOGICAL WORK

JOURNAL OF ROMAN ARCHAEOLOGY

SUPPLEMENTARY SERIES NUMBER 24

General Editor: J. H. Humphrey

Assistant Editor: D. S. Stone

ROMAN LONDON
RECENT ARCHAEOLOGICAL WORK

including papers given at a seminar held at
The Museum of London on 16 November, 1996

edited by Bruce Watson

with contributions by

N. Bateman, T. Brigham, M. Fulford, M. Hutchinson,
M. Millett, B. Rankov, L. Rayner, K. Rielly,
P. Rowsome, D. Sankey, F. Seeley, J. Sidell,
A. Wardle, B. Watson, A. Westman, & B. Yule

Portsmouth, Rhode Island
1998

Addresses of contributors

M. Fulford, Department of Archaeology, University of Reading, Whiteknights, Reading, RG6 2AA

M. Millett, Department of Archaeology, University of Durham, South Road, Durham, DH1 3LE.

B. Rankov, Royal Holloway, Egham, Surrey, TWE20 0EX.

B. Yule, 'Long Marston', Tockwith Rd, Marston, N. Yorks, Y05 8PQ.

All other contributors: Museum of London Archaeology Service, Walker House, 87 Queen Victoria Street, London EC4V 4AB.

Credits

The Conference on which this volume is based was organised for the Council for British Archaeology, Mid Anglia Group, by Peter Clayton, chairman; he was assisted in this task by Derek Hills and Robin Densem.

The graphics for publication were produced by Kikar Singh, the photographs (except fig. 15) by Andy Chopping and Maggie Cox, figures 16 and 17 by Dave Bentley, and the papers were edited by Tony Dyson, all of MoLAS.

Thanks are also due to the City of London Archaeological Trust for a publication grant which funded the production of figs. 2 and 3.

ISBN 1-887829-24-5
ISSN 1063-4304 (for the supplementary series)

This and other supplements to the Journal of Roman Archaeology may be ordered from:
JRA, 95 Peleg Road, Portsmouth, RI 02871, U.S.A.
Orders may also be placed by e-mail: jra@wsii.com
telephone (USA) 401 683 1955, or telefax (USA) 401 683 1975 (fax only)
or from
Oxbow Books, Park End Place, Oxford, OX1 1HN, England
telephone (U.K.) 1865-241 249, telefax (U.K.) 1865-794 449
This supplement may also be ordered from
The Museum of London, Walker House, 87 Queen Victoria St., London EC4V 4AB.

TABLE OF CONTENTS

FREQUENTLY CITED ABBREVIATION

Interpreting London   J. Bird, M. Hassall and H. Sheldon (edd.), *Interpreting Roman London: papers in memory of Hugh Chapman* (Oxbow Monograph 58, Oxford 1996)

All dates in this book are A.D. unless otherwise indicated.

LIST OF FIGURES

Introduction:
London as capital?
Martin Millett

The papers presented here are based on those given at a day-seminar organized by the Mid Anglia Group of the Council for British Archaeology and held at the Museum of London on 16 November, 1996. Their aim was to review recent archaeological work on Roman London. It was evident on the day that the richness of the information presented justified publication, especially as the final reports on the various projects will not be available for several years. This introduction is based on my concluding remarks offered at the meeting. As then, I do not now wish to summarize the papers in any conventional sense; instead, I would like to discuss one aspect of the archaeology of London from a broader perspective.[1]

It is important to emphasize one point about the extent of our present knowledge of the archaeology of the Roman town. London is now much more extensively explored than most other Roman towns in W Europe; although excavations since the 1970s have been the product of the pressures of development, and have sometimes been limited in scope, the aggregate of the information gathered places London amongst the best known Roman towns.[2] This suggests that problems of understanding are most likely to result from the asking of inappropriate questions rather than from an absence of good data. As it seems unlikely that there are going to be many more large-scale excavations in London in the next few years, it is important that, whilst publishing reports on past excavations, we formulate new research questions which will help us better to understand London within the broader context of the Roman world. As a background to this, I will make some observations about

---

1   For my previous views on Roman London see "Evaluating Roman London," *Arch J* 151 (1994) 427-35, and "Characterizing Roman London," in *Interpreting London* 33-39. In the present collection Roman London is described as a town since its precise urban status is uncertain.

2   For Gaul, compare the evidence in R. Bedon, R. Chevallier and P. Pinon, *Architecture et urbanisme en Gaule romaine*, 2: *L'urbanisme* (Paris 1988) and, for Spain, *The Hispano-Roman town* (Exhib. Cat., Ministerio de Cultura, Barcelona 1993) and W. Trillmich and P. Zanker (edd.), *Stadtbild und ideologie* (Munich 1990).

Martin Millett

London's rôle as a provincial capital and draw a few comparisons with other major sites in W Europe.

London as a provincial capital?

London's dominance within the settlement-system of Roman Britain is undeniable. Its absolute size (130 ha excluding Southwark), and the manner in which it acts as the focal point for the road-system within Britain, show how dominant it was, whilst the shape of the rank-size graph of towns from Roman Britain[3] suggests that it was also economically paramount. However, these features do not necessarily mean that it was the provincial capital: indeed, I think we need to deconstruct this term.

The evidence for London's status is comparatively limited.[4] The city seems to have been founded *de novo* around A.D. 50, perhaps by traders from other provinces. It experienced a very rapid growth before its destruction in the Boudiccan revolt of 60-61. At that date it did not have the status of a chartered town and was perhaps a *conventus civium Romanorum*. There is some evidence that the settlement remained legally subservient to Canterbury at least down to the 2nd c.[5] In the early years after the conquest, Colchester had become an important centre of the province and the establishment of the Colonia Claudia Victricensis Camulodunensium in 49, together with the dedication of a temple to the deified Claudius (after 54), should probably be taken as evidence that it was to be the chief town of the province, the centre of the provincial council and imperial cult.

In the wake of the Boudiccan revolt, important officials were based in London, as illustrated by the tombstone of the procurator Classicianus (*RIB* 12) and other inscribed items. This and other evidence recently summarized by Hassall have led to the conclusion that London superseded Colchester to become the provincial capital, perhaps by the later 1st c.[6] Indeed, a major town-house excavated in the 1960-70s has been identified as the governor's palace.[7]

---

3   M. Millett, *The Romanization of Britain* (London 1990) ill. 62.
4   Millett, "Characterizing Roman London" (supra n.1) and J. J. Wilkes, "The status of Roman London," ibid. 27-32.
5   Millett, "Characterizing Roman London" ibid. 35.
6   M. W. C. Hassall, "London as a provincial capital," ibid.
7   P. Marsden, "Excavation of a Roman palace site in London, 1961-72," *TransLonMiddxArchSoc* 26 (1975) 1-103, but see now G. Milne, "A palace

The conclusion that London became a provincial capital seems to me to be one that should be challenged both on general grounds and on the basis of the specific evidence used. Roman provincial government involved the juxtaposition of military, judicial, financial, and administrative rôles. The governor oversaw an essentially federal system of quasi-autonomous self-governing cities. He took a lead in military, judicial, and religious affairs at the provincial level. A counterbalance to his power was provided by the provincial procurator, who was responsible for the financial supervision of the province. With a separation of functions between self-governing cities, a provincial priesthood, a governor, and a procurator, there is no reason why all the rôles should have been exercised from the same place. Indeed, the concept of a provincial capital may itself be anachronistic and too heavily influenced by modern concepts of the nation state. Several of the above rôles, at the most, might have existed in a single place.

A wide range of evidence also supports the idea that in the early Roman empire power was exercised on a personal rather than an institutional basis.[8] Thus, government was where the governor was at any particular moment. In the context of earlier Roman Britain, the governor would have been peripatetic, being present with the army when it was campaigning, at other times moving amongst the *civitates* to deal with issues of administration and justice on a face-to-face basis. He would have had his own entourage of seconded soldiers and personal clients many of whom would have moved around with him. When at military bases they would probably have lived in the commanding officer's house as his guests. While on tour, they would have stayed as guests of civilian magistrates or other local luminaries. If the governor did have his own residence, it seems more likely to have been personal rather than official property, and thus indistinguishable from the houses of other members of the provincial élite. When in London, the chief town of the province, he may have resided in the commanding officer's house in the fort at Cripplegate, or in a private house, whether his own or that of another. One could not identify his own residence on archaeological grounds alone, and the search for a governor's palace seems to me misguided. The presence of members of the governor's staff based at London[9] does not seem to

---

disproved: reassessing the provincial governor's presence in 1st century London," in *Interpreting London* 49-55.

8   F. G. B. Millar, *The emperor in the Roman world* (London 1977).

9   Hassall (supra n.6).

demonstrate any more than that London was the largest town of the province, on the route from Rome, and so a place where a major governmental presence was inevitable.

The other half of the provincial administration, the provincial procurator's office, certainly had its base in London, presumably again because it was the principal port of entry and the largest town. The provincial procurator's office needed a permanent base for the housing of tax records and so forth, and there seems little question that this was to be found in London. I doubt, however, that this means that we should label London as the provincial capital. It seems that Colchester retained an equal claim to importance within the province as the centre for the imperial cult.

The term 'capital' is a modern construct. I fear its use obscures attempts at understanding the differing rôles of London and other towns at various stages in the development of the province.

Inter-provincial comparisons

Having deconstructed the concept of provincial capital we should turn briefly to draw some comparisons with other cities in the western empire. The sites which have generally been considered capitals of other provinces are shown in fig. 1 with table 1. Although I do not have sufficient space to be able to discuss them in detail, a series of observations and comparisons can be made.

Table 1
Towns in the western empire usually considered as provincial capitals (fig. 1)

Gallia

G. Narbonensis	Narbonne	Colonia Julia Paterna Claudia Narbo Martius Decumanorum (*colonia* founded 118 B.C.)
G. Lugdunensis	Lyon	Lugdunum, Colonia Copia Felix Munatia Augusta (Caesarian colony) (seat of Council of the Three Gauls)
G. Aquitania	Bordeaux	Burdigalia (Flavian *municipium*)
G. Belgica	Reims	Durocortorum Remorum (*civitas* capital, not chartered town) (residence of propraetorian governor)
	Trier	Colonia Augusta Treverorum (*colonia* by A.D. 138) (seat of *fiscus* of the three provinces of the Germanies and G. Belgica)

Hispaniae

H. Baetica	Córdoba	Corduba, Colonia Patricia (*colonia latina* probably founded 152 B.C.)
H. Lusitania	Mérida	Colonia Augusta Emerita (Augustan colony)
H. Tarraconensis	Tarragona	Tarraco, Colonia Julia Urbs Triumphalis Tarraconensis (Augustan colony) (seat of provincial council of the provinces of Spain)

Germania

| G. Superior | Mainz | Mogontiacum (*municipium* attested only in A.D. 355) (also a legionary base) |
| G. Inferior | Cologne | Colonia Claudia Ara Agrippinensis (*colonia* founded A.D. 50) |

Fig.1. Map of western Roman empire during later 1st c. A.D., showing sites usually considered to be provincial capitals (for details see Table 1).

London's size (at 130 ha excluding Southwark) is greater than the average,[10] although the proportion of its area taken up by public buildings and its total of both monumental structures and inscriptions appears modest. This supports the idea that the character of Roman urbanism varied greatly across the provinces and that the growth of London was the result of processes different to those influencing other provinces. I would infer that its rôle as the entrepôt of a heavily militarized province was particularly influential, comparable with centres like Cologne and Mainz but in contrast with other centres.

We may note that the difficulty in distinguishing which cities might have acted as the principal centres of provinces is not confined to Britain, supporting the conclusion that to label centres as provincial capitals may be incorrect. In some provinces, cities (e.g., Tarraco) acted as the seat of the provincial council and as the cult centre as well as serving from time to time as the governor's place of residence. Elsewhere, the situation is more uncertain. In Gallia Belgica the governor seems to have been resident at Reims, but the *fiscus* of the provinces of Belgica and the two Germanies was based at Trier (which later became an imperial residence). We may also note that there is no single pattern of status associated with such towns: whilst many were colonies or were raised to that status, the pattern is by no means uniform. Mainz, the town perhaps most similar to London, remained a legionary base and is of uncertain civic status.[11] This supports the idea that we need to rethink varying urban functions across the western empire and not simply assume that by applying labels like 'provincial capital' we provide explanations.

Recent archaeological work on London is providing new sources of evidence for our understanding of urbanism in the western empire as a whole. The papers which follow demonstrate something of the richness and give brief insights into the interpretative discussions which are in progress. The mass of evidence now available from London should be of help to scholars working on cities in other parts of the empire.[12]

---

10   The other sites for which I have data are: Narbonne *c.*100 ha; Bordeaux *c.*125 ha; Trier *c.*81 ha; Mérida *c.*70 ha; Tarraco *c.*70 ha. For comparison, the area of Rome in the Augustan period has been estimated as 1783 ha (N. Morley, *Metropolis and hinterland* [Cambridge 1996] 34).

11   John Mann (pers. comm.) notes that Ammianus' attribution of the title *municipium* needs to be treated with caution.

12   See the bibliography provided in *Interpreting London*.

A brief history of archaeological exploration in Roman London

Bruce Watson

London's skyline today is dominated by tall, modern buildings, and there are few visible signs that it was an ancient city. Yet ironically it was their construction that revealed the remains of the buried Roman town, and it is only the frequency and extent of redevelopment which has resulted in so extensive an exploration of the Roman town.

For centuries property development within the modern city has revealed fragments of the Roman precursor. As early as 1595, during the construction of a cellar, a Roman 'pavement' was found 15 feet (4.57 m) below ground level at the corner of Bread Street and Cheapside, indicating the depth of build-up of archaeological deposits even before the modern period.[1] The volume of archaeological discoveries increased dramatically during the 19th c. with the construction of sewers, railway stations, and commercial buildings with deep basements. These activities were observed by a number of antiquaries,[2] the most famous of whom was Charles Roach Smith, whose collection of finds became in 1856 the nucleus of the British Museum's Romano-British collection.[3] The 19th-c. development of London revealed a number of impressive mosaic pavements — Leadenhall street in 1803, Old Broad Street in 1854, and Bucklersbury in 1869.[4] From c.1890 to 1912, Dr Philip Norman and Francis W. Reader carried out watching briefs on a number of redevelopments. It was their publications which provided the first accurate plans of many important features such as the Roman town wall and the Walbrook stream[5] (figs. 2-3).

---

1   J. Stow (ed. C. L. Kingsford), *A survey of London* 1 (Oxford 1971) 345.

2   P. Marsden, "The beginnings of archaeology in the City of London," in *Interpreting London* 11-18; R. Merrifield, *The Roman city of London* (London 1965) 1-25.

3   C. R. Smith, *Catalogue of the Museum of London Antiquities* (London 1854); M. Rhodes, *Some aspects of the contribution to British archaeology of Charles Roach Smith (1806-90)* (PhD thesis, University of London 1993).

4   Merrifield (supra n.2) 246, 288, 289.

5   P. Norman and F. W. Reader, "Recent discoveries in connection with Roman London," *Archaeologia* 60 (1906) 169-250; "Further discoveries relating to Roman London 1906-12," ibid. 63 (1912) 257-344.

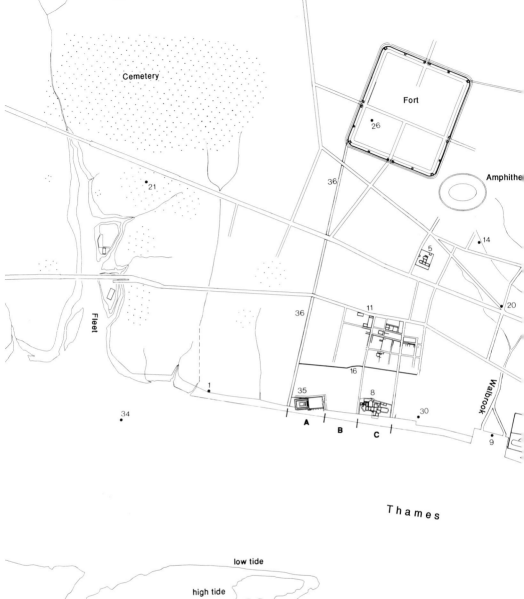

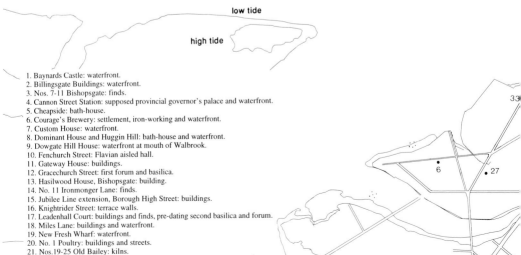

1. Baynards Castle: waterfront.
2. Billingsgate Buildings: waterfront.
3. Nos. 7-11 Bishopsgate: finds.
4. Cannon Street Station: supposed provincial governor's palace and waterfront.
5. Cheapside: bath-house.
6. Courage's Brewery: settlement, iron-working and waterfront.
7. Custom House: waterfront.
8. Dominant House and Huggin Hill: bath-house and waterfront.
9. Dowgate Hill House: waterfront at mouth of Walbrook.
10. Fenchurch Street: Flavian aisled hall.
11. Gateway House: buildings.
12. Gracechurch Street: first forum and basilica.
13. Hasilwood House, Bishopsgate: building.
14. No. 11 Ironmonger Lane: finds.
15. Jubilee Line extension, Borough High Street: buildings.
16. Knightrider Street: terrace walls.
17. Leadenhall Court: buildings and finds, pre-dating second basilica and forum.
18. Miles Lane: buildings and waterfront.
19. New Fresh Wharf: waterfront.
20. No. 1 Poultry: buildings and streets.
21. Nos.19-25 Old Bailey: kilns.

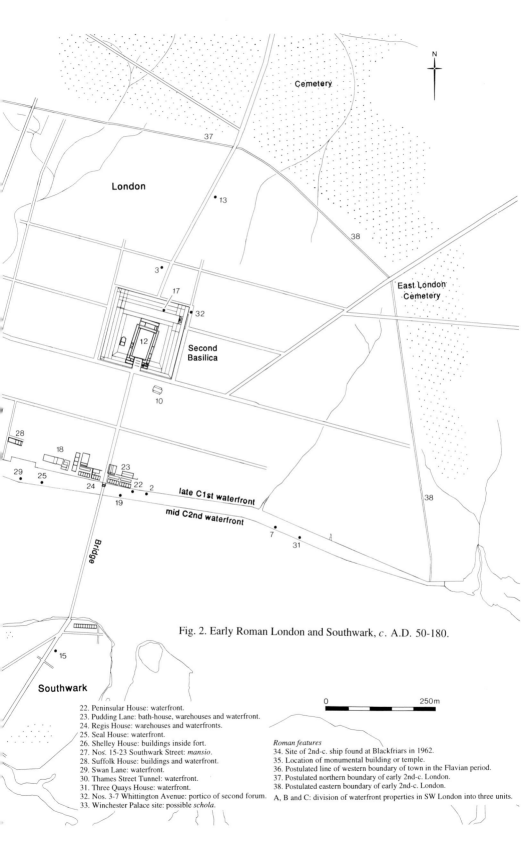

N

Cemetery

London

37

• 13

38

East London
Cemetery

3 •

17

• 32

12

Second
Basilica

10

28

18

29   25

23

24   22   2

19

late C1st waterfront

mid C2nd waterfront

7

31

38

Bridge

15

Fig. 2. Early Roman London and Southwark, *c*. A.D. 50-180.

Southwark

22. Peninsular House: waterfront.
23. Pudding Lane: bath-house, warehouses and waterfront.
24. Regis House: warehouses and waterfronts.
25. Seal House: waterfront.
26. Shelley House: buildings inside fort.
27. Nos. 15-23 Southwark Street: *mansio*.
28. Suffolk House: buildings and waterfront.
29. Swan Lane: waterfront.
30. Thames Street Tunnel: waterfront.
31. Three Quays House: waterfront.
32. Nos. 3-7 Whittington Avenue: portico of second forum.
33. Winchester Palace site: possible *schola*.

0   250m

Roman features
34. Site of 2nd-c. ship found at Blackfriars in 1962.
35. Location of monumental building or temple.
36. Postulated line of western boundary of town in the Flavian period.
37. Postulated northern boundary of early 2nd-c. London.
38. Postulated eastern boundary of early 2nd-c. London.
A, B and C: division of waterfront properties in SW London into three units.

Fig.2 (previous pages) shows natural streams, the extent of major buildings, and the line of the late 1st- and mid 2nd-c. waterfronts, to show the general extent of reclamation of the Thames foreshore. This stretch of the Thames estuary was tidal during the Roman period; in Southwark settlement was restricted to flood-free areas of higher ground, and surrounded by creeks and mud-flats. Some elements of the road network shown here are projected from fragmentary observations. The exact extent of the various extra-mural cemeteries is unknown. The precise lines of town boundaries during this period are also uncertain; the existence of the Flavian W boundary of the town (site 36) is postulated from the existence of a number of small cemeteries further west.

In the 1920s, Roman London was surveyed by the Royal Commission on Historical Monuments (RCHM), and the resulting publication provides an invaluable gazetteer.[6] It demonstrated the need for building sites to be watched by archaeologists during redevelopment. In 1929 Gerald C. Dunning was appointed by the Society of Antiquaries and Guildhall Museum to record archaeological findings on all building sites. Dunning's work resulted in the identification of the Hadrianic fire (c.120-130).[7] In 1934 Frank Cottrill took over from Dunning as city archaeologist and in the following year he discovered within one of the 4th-c. bastions on Tower Hill an inscribed fragment of the tombstone of Classicianus, procurator of Britain during the late 1st c. (another fragment had been found in the same bastion in 1852).[8]

Wartime bombing and V-rocket attacks on London in 1940-44 resulted in extensive destruction, and from 1946 to 1968 Prof. W. F. Grimes directed numerous excavations on such bomb sites in advance of redevelopment. For the first time, archaeologists undertook controlled and scientific excavations of threatened sites instead of merely observing their destruction during redevelopment. As Grimes's resources were limited, often he was able to excavate only small portions of the available sites. His two most important achievements were the identification of the Cripplegate fort and the excavation of the Mithraeum in

---

6   R. C. H. M., *Roman London* (London 1928).
7   G. C. Dunning, "Two fires of Roman London," *AntJ* 25 (1945) 48-77. The dating evidence for the Hadrianic fire was based on the assemblage of Samian ware found within the fire débris at Regis House in 1929-31. Excavation of the rest of this site in the redevelopment of 1994-96 provided a unique opportunity to re-examine the dating evidence for this fire (T. Brigham *et al.*, "Current archaeological work at Regis House," *London Archaeologist* 8 [1996] 29-38 [pt. 1], 63-69 [pt. 2]).
8   Merrifield (supra n.2) 320; S. Ireland, *Roman Britain: a source book* (2nd ed., London 1996) 71.

1954[9] (fig. 2; fig. 3, site 27). On bomb sites in Southwark the first controlled excavations within the Roman settlement were directed by Kathleen Kenyon in 1945-47.[10] This was the start of a long involvement by Surrey Archaeological Society in the organising and publication of Southwark excavations.

In the 1950-60s, several archaeologists from the Guildhall Museum carried out watching briefs on sites which were being destroyed during redevelopment.[11] Resources were generally insufficient to undertake controlled excavation, but many important discoveries were made. They included the excavation of two boats, one in Southwark and another at Blackfriars,[12] and three bath-houses,[13] while work at Cannon Street Station (1961-71) led to the identification of a palace complex, interpreted as the provincial governor's palace[14] (fig. 2, sites 4, 5, 8, 34; fig. 3, site 3).

---

9   W. F. Grimes, *The excavation of Roman and mediaeval London* (London 1968) 15-39, 98-117; J. M. C. Toynbee, *The Roman art treasures from the Temple of Mithras* (London & Middx Arch. Soc. Special Paper 7, 1986); Grimes never produced final reports on his excavations before his death in 1988, but this work has now been done by John Shepherd of the Museum of London and monographs on the fort and Mithraeum (id., *The Temple of Mithras, London, Excavations by W. F. Grimes and A. Williams at the Walbrook* [English Heritage Archaeological Report]) are forthcoming.

10   K. M. Kenyon, *Excavations in Southwark* (Research Paper of the Surrey Arch. Soc. 5, 1959). See Westman's paper below for details of recent Southwark publications.

11   I. Noël Hume, "Into the jaws of death ... walked one," in J. Bird, H. Chapman, J. Clark (edd.), *Collectanea Londiniensia: studies presented to Ralph Merrifield* (London & Middx Arch. Soc. Special Paper 2, 1978) 7-22; J. Schofield, *Archive guide to Guildhall Museum sites 1924-73* (unpublished site gazetteer produced by the Museum of London, 1994).

12   P. Marsden, *Ships of the port of London (first to eleventh centuries A.D.,* (English Heritage Archaeological Report 3, 1994) 33-10; G. Milne, "Blackfriars ship 1: Romano-Celtic, Gallo-Roman or Classis Britannica?" *IJNA* 25 (1996) 234-38.

13   P. Marsden, "Two Roman public baths in London," *TransLonMiddxArchSoc* 27 (1976) 2-70.

14   P. Marsden, "The excavation of a Roman palace site in London 1961-62," *TransLonMiddxArchSoc* 26 (1975) 1-102. Marsden's interpretation has recently been disputed by G. Milne, "A palace disproved: reassessing the provincial governor's presence in 1st-century London," in *Interpreting London* 149-55. Until the DUA excavations of 1988-89 are published, giving important new information on the plan, phasing, and function of this com-

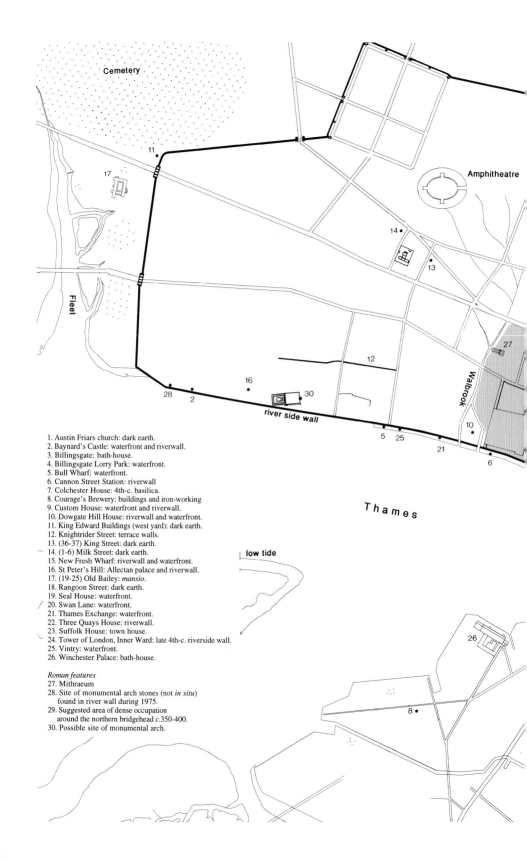

Cemetery

Amphitheatre

11

17

14 •

13

Fleet

27

12

Walbrook

16

28   2

30

10

river side wall

5   25

21

6

Thames

low tide

26

8 •

1. Austin Friars church: dark earth.
2. Baynard's Castle: waterfront and riverwall.
3. Billingsgate: bath-house.
4. Billingsgate Lorry Park: waterfront.
5. Bull Wharf: waterfront.
6. Cannon Street Station: riverwall
7. Colchester House: 4th-c. basilica.
8. Courage's Brewery: buildings and iron-working
9. Custom House: waterfront and riverwall.
10. Dowgate Hill House: riverwall and waterfront.
11. King Edward Buildings (west yard): dark earth.
12. Knightrider Street: terrace walls.
13. (36-37) King Street: dark earth.
14. (1-6) Milk Street: dark earth.
15. New Fresh Wharf: riverwall and waterfront.
16. St Peter's Hill: Allectan palace and riverwall.
17. (19-25) Old Bailey: *mansio*.
18. Rangoon Street: dark earth.
19. Seal House: waterfront.
20. Swan Lane: waterfront.
21. Thames Exchange: waterfront.
22. Three Quays House: riverwall.
23. Suffolk House: town house.
24. Tower of London, Inner Ward: late 4th-c. riverside wall.
25. Vintry: waterfront.
26. Winchester Palace: bath-house.

Roman features
27. Mithraeum
28. Site of monumental arch stones (not *in situ*)
    found in river wall during 1975.
29. Suggested area of dense occupation
    around the northern bridgehead *c*.350-400.
30. Possible site of monumental arch.

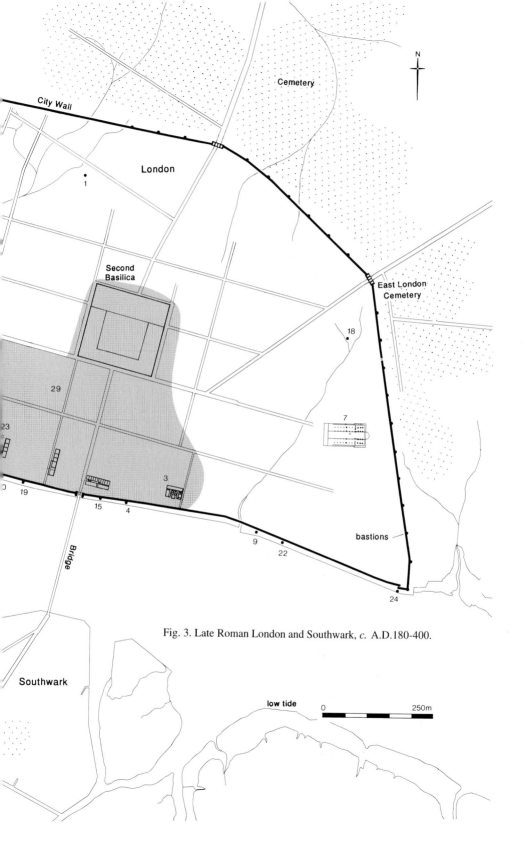

N

Cemetery

City Wall

London

1

Second
Basilica

East London
Cemetery

18

29

7

23

3

19

15   4

9

22

bastions

Bridge

24

Fig. 3. Late Roman London and Southwark, *c.* A.D.180-400.

Southwark

low tide   0   250m

Fig.3 (previous pages) shows the position of major buildings, roads, extent of the extra-mural cemeteries, line of the town wall, and position of the gates. The town wall was constructed between *c*.180 and 225. The early 2nd-c. fort was apparently demolished about the time the town walls were constructed, but its N and W walls were retained and incorporated within the town wall. In the late 4th c. a series of bastions was added to the eastern stretch of the wall, and a wide ditch was excavated along the entire circuit. The last phase of water-front or quayside was constructed during the early to mid 3rd c., at which time the river frontage was still undefended. Later in the 3rd c. (*c*.255-275) a masonry river-wall was constructed along the entire river-front. The extreme E end of the river-wall was rebuilt during the late 4th c. (site 24). It is not known if there were water-gates along the river-wall providing access to the river. The exact extent of the occupied area of the town in 350-400 is uncertain (site 29), though the main focus of settlement was certainly around the northern bridgehead. Late Roman Southwark possessed no defences. The date when the bridge over the Thames, linking Southwark and London, went out of use is unknown.

In 1973, in recognition that the city's archaeology was often being destroyed without record, the Guildhall Museum formed the Department of Urban Archaeology (DUA) to undertake rescue excavations on sites threatened with redevelopment and destruction.[15] The work of the DUA over the next 18 years included the investigation of the Roman port and its timber quays;[16] the late-Roman riverside wall[17] and further work on a number of previously excavated structures including the bath-house at Huggin Hill;[18] the second basilica;[19] and the

---

plex of monumental buildings and waterfronts, there seems little point in attempting to reinterpret the earlier discoveries.

15   In 1975 the Guildhall Museum merged with the London Museum to form the present Museum of London. The results of the last 20 years' fieldwork are shown in the Museum's new Roman gallery, opened in 1996.

16   See Brigham's paper below and G. Milne, *The port of London* (London 1985).

17   C. Hill, M. Millett and T. Blagg, *The Roman riverside wall and monumental arch in London* (London & Middx Arch. Soc. Special Paper 3, 1980). The construction of the river-wall is now dated to *c*.255-75 by dendrochronological analysis of its oak-pile foundations (H. Sheldon and I. Tyers, "Recent dendrochronological work in Southwark and its implications," *London Archaeologist* 4 [1983] 355-61).

18   P. Rowsome, "The Huggin Hill Baths and other baths buildings in Roman London: barometers of the town's changing circumstances?," JRA Suppl. (forthcoming).

19   T. Brigham, "A reassessment of the second basilica in London, A.D. 100-400," *Britannia* 21 (1990) 53-97; G. Milne (ed.), *From Roman basilica to medieval market* (London 1992) 1-33, 51-113.

town defences.[20] Open-area excavations produced large assemblages of finds and details of vernacular buildings.[21] The excavation of water-logged sites produced unique finds and environmental assemblages,[22] along with thousands of timbers, including fragments of timber-framed buildings.[23] In 1987, excavation of the site of the mediaeval chapel at Guildhall revealed part of an amphitheatre[24] (figs. 2-3).

In 1983, several existing archaeological units covering the Greater London area were amalgamated to form the Department of Greater London Archaeology (DGLA) of the Museum of London. During the late 1980s, there was an unprecedented amount of redevelopment in London, resulting in numerous rescue excavations by the DGLA and DUA.[25] They included an intensive programme of work in Roman Southwark and within the Roman cemeteries east of the city[26] (fig. 2, sites 6, 27, 33).

In 1991, the DGLA and DUA were amalgamated to form the Museum of London Archaeology Service (MoLAS). Since 1991 there have been large scale excavations in the city in the area of the amphitheatre

20 J. Maloney, "Recent work on London's defences," in J. Maloney and B. Hobley (edd.), *Roman urban defences in the west* (CBA Res. Rep. 51, 1983) 96-117; D. Sankey and A. Stephenson, "Recent work on London's defences," in V. A. Maxfield and M. J. Dobson (edd.), *Roman frontier studies, Proc. 15th Int. Cong. Roman Frontier Studies* (Exeter 1991) 117-24.

21 D. Perring, "The buildings," in D. Perring and S. Roskams, with P. Allen, *Early development of Roman London west of the Walbrook* (CBA Res. Rep. 70, 1991) 67-107.

22 See papers by Rayner and Seeley and by Wardle below; I. M. Betts, "Procuratorial tile stamps from London," *Britannia* 26 (1995) 207-29; C. Maloney with D. de Moulins, *The upper Walbrook valley in the Roman period* (CBA Res. Rep. 69, 1990).

23 D. Goodburn, "A Roman timber-framed building tradition," *ArchJ* 148 (1991) 182-204.

24 N. Bateman, "The discovery of London's amphitheatre: excavations at the Old Art Gallery site 1987-88 and 1990," *London Archaeologist* 6 (1990) 232-41.

25 See the papers by Westman and Yule and Rankov below for the 1980s Southwark excavations, with forthcoming publications.

26 B. Barber, D. Bowsher and K. Whittaker, "Recent excavations of a cemetery of Londinium," *Britannia* 21 (1990) 1-12. The east London Roman cemetery is soon to be published as a monograph (see Sidell and Rielly's paper below for a discussion of the faunal material from the east London cemeteries). For an up-to-date summary of all the London and Southwark cemeteries, see J. Hall, "The cemeteries of Roman London: a review," *Interpreting London* 57-84.

(1992-96);[27] at No.1 Poultry (1994-96);[28] and Regis House (1994-96). The Regis House excavations were the second phase of work on that site, following a watching brief carried out by Dunning in 1929-31 when the site was last redeveloped.[29] A number of smaller excavations (such as Colchester House [1992][30]) and site evaluations have also been carried out since 1991.[31] In Southwark the extension of the Jubilee Line underground railway in 1994-95 necessitated a major programme of excavations[32] (fig. 2, sites 15, 20, 24; fig. 3, site 7).

Further major excavations within the Roman town are unlikely, for two reasons. First, on the majority of proposed developments, most if not all of the archaeological deposits have already been destroyed by the construction of existing buildings. Second, following the recognition that London's archaeology is a finite and precious resource, the city's planning authority now expects redevelopment proposals to provide solutions with limited archaeological impact — i.e., as far as possible allowing deposits to remain undisturbed.[33] Yet even if we dig up less of Roman London in the future, many of the excavations which have been carried out since the 1970s remain to be analysed and published, and the resulting wealth of new information is certain to transform our view of Roman London during the next decade.

---

27 See Bateman's paper below and his "The London amphitheatre: excavations 1987-1996," *Britannia* 28 (1997).

28 See Rowsome's paper below and his "Number 1 Poultry: evaluation and phase one excavations," *London Archaeologist* 7 (1995) 371-37. An interim report on Number 1 Poultry is now published: M. Birch, D. Lees, J. Hill, P. Rowsome, S. Jones and P. Treveil, "Number 1 Poultry — the main excavation: Roman sequence," *London Archaeologist* 8 (1997) 127-36.

29 T. Brigham *et al.* (supra n.7).

30 See Sankey's paper below.

31 Site evaluations can produce important new archaeological information (cf. Watson's paper below).

32 See Hutchinson's paper below.

33 *Planning policy guidance note 16: archaeology and planning, Department of the Environment* (London 1990); *City of London unitary development plan, Corporation of London Dept. of Planning* (1994) 192-95. Some features of the Roman town such as the town walls, the Cannon Street palace, and the amphitheatre are now government-protected Scheduled Ancient Monuments and prior consent for any work or excavation on them must be obtained from the Department of National Heritage.

The port of Roman London

Trevor Brigham

This paper attempts to summarise the development of the Roman port in London, between 50 and 270, briefly discussing the suburb on the south bank (Southwark) before turning to other aspects of the port.[1]

Origins

Londinium was built on two hills which were divided by the Walbrook and fell to the Thames in a series of post-glacial gravel terraces cut by several small streams and springs. The town probably originated not long before 50 as a modest settlement around the lowest possible bridging point on the Thames.[2] A suburb probably developed at an early point on the south bank. This location also proved to be a suitable interchange for land, river, and sea-borne traffic (fig. 2).

The topography of the bridgehead was modified almost immediately with the creation of extended gravel terraces. From 52,[3] the lowest of these terraces was progressively protected by revetments which, after a decade or so, extended across the river frontage of most of the town. The new embankments were simple affairs normally consisting of piles hammered into the foreshore and supporting plank cladding. Low wattle revetments and clusters of timber piles, which may represent the remains of ancillary structures such as silt traps, jetties, or mooring posts, stretched across the foreshore to the south. In some areas, the foreshore itself was consolidated to form a hard surface, ideal for

---

1   Earlier discussions of the port have been published by G. Milne, *The port of Roman London* (London 1985) and T. Brigham, "The late Roman waterfront in London," *Britannia* 21 (1990) 99-183. References to most of the sites discussed in this paper are found in these works, unless otherwise stated.

2   The Roman bridge was built opposite the eastern of the two hills in roughly the same place as the Saxon and mediaeval bridges. A multi-period study of London Bridge (currently in preparation) concludes that the earliest semi-permanent structure was probably constructed shortly after the invasion in 43. With several phases of rebuilding, the bridge probably survived the end of the Roman period, and possibly beyond.

3   This date was obtained by dendrochronological analysis of timbers from a revetment excavated at Regis House, King William Street, 1994-96 (fig. 2, site 24). This excavation is summarised in T. Brigham, B. Watson *et al.*, "Current archaeological work at Regis House in the City of London," *London Archaeologist* 8 (1996) 31-37 (pt. 1), 63-68 (pt. 2).

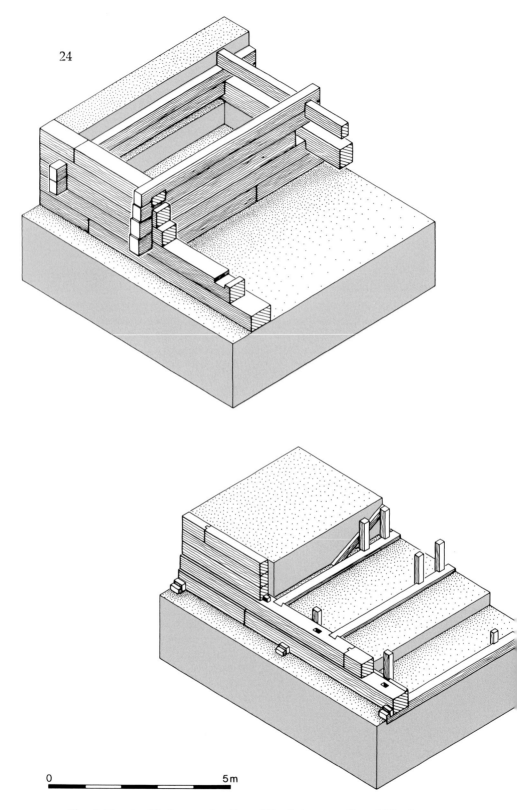

0   5m

Fig. 4. Top: typified reconstruction of the 1st-c. quay from Miles Lane;
Bottom: typified reconstruction of 2nd-c. quay from Swan Lane.

grounding flat-bottomed rivercraft. Contemporary buildings lay on the terraces above the waterfront; in the first decade of the port's development none can be identified as a warehouse or another structure having a direct connection with the river.

Development of the port

The first port facility was modest: the impetus for growth came with the reconstruction of *Londinium* following the Boudiccan revolt of 60-61. In the aftermath of the revolt, a roughly 30-year programme of quay building was undertaken as part of a much larger effort to restore the burnt-out town. The driving force may have been the procurator Julius Alpinus Classicianus, who held one of the few offices capable of co-ordinating such an ambitious project.

The new wharf was built in sections, each around 120-30 m long, beginning in 63-64 immediately upstream of the bridge.[4] It consisted of a massive quay 2.0 m high constructed in front of the existing embankments. This quay had a solid frontage of squared oak beams retained by tiebacks running to a rear wall of timber and forming a series of infilled boxes (fig. 4). By *c*.90, three further sections had been completed, one downstream of the bridge, and the final two to either side of the Walbrook, creating a balanced wharf with the bridge and the Walbrook as twin foci.[5] The discovery of a strip of scale armour (*lorica squamata*) and leather fragments of a military tent in the infill of the quay at Regis House (fig. 2, site 24) strongly suggests that military labour was employed. A stamp on the end of one quay timber has recently

---

4   This secure date was established by dendrochronological dating of a large sample of timbers from the site at Regis House, King William Street.

5   The first section included quays recorded next to the bridge at Regis House (1929-31 and 1994-96) and the neighbouring site of Miles Lane (1920, 1979), where the structure probably terminated on the line of the channel of a stream (fig. 2, site 18). The second section upstream of the bridge consisted of a landing stage built *c*.80 at the sites at Pudding Lane/Peninsular House (fig. 2, sites 22, 23: excavated 1981 and 1979), ending in the east where it joined a revetment at Billingsgate Buildings (fig. 2, site 2: 1974). The third section to the east of the Walbrook consists of quays recorded at Cannon Street Station (fig. 2, site 4: 1988) and Suffolk House (fig. 2, site 28: 1996), where it terminated next to a marshy inlet. The final section west of the Walbrook was recorded in a telecommunications tunnel beneath Upper Thames Street (fig. 2, site 30: 1978), terminating opposite the church of St James Garlickhithe, where it joined a piled embankment recorded further west at Dominant House (fig. 2, site 8: 1988).

Trevor Brigham

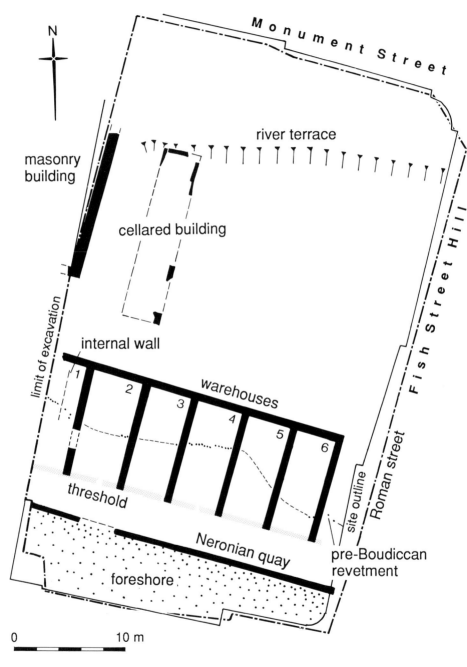

Fig. 5. The Neronian quay and associated buildings at Regis House.

been read as TRAECAVG which may attest to the presence of a Thracian unit.[6]

The construction programme included the creation of a series of level terraces for building. Springs and small streams encountered were either tapped for domestic use or diverted through the quay into the river. Several public buildings were also constructed, and perhaps encouraged private development which followed more haphazardly. At Regis House, a warehouse block was erected as an integral part of the wharf, and was divided internally into at least 6 separate two-storeyed bays, each 4.5 m wide and 10 m long (fig. 5). Grooved thresholds supported shutters or folding doors opening on to the wharf which was 4.5 m wide. The warehouse was used both for storage and workshops: small glass objects were produced in the fourth bay,[7] which may later have served as a mosaicist's workshop or store. A neighbouring bay harboured a cache of three Vespasianic lead ingots hidden beneath an early floor (fig. 6).[8] A later occupant of this bay dealt in turned stone products, including a fine calcite vase. After 95 a block of warehouses similar to those at Regis House was constructed downstream of the bridge at Pudding Lane/Peninsula House (fig. 2, sites 22, 23).

The quay on the east bank of the Walbrook was probably built to provide river access for the structure identified as the Governor's Palace (fig. 2, site 4).[9] At this early period, although the large building

---

6   Only one example of this type of stamp was recorded on the site. The provisional reading by M. W. C. Hassall is [...]*IRAECAVG*[...], *Thraec(orum) Aug(usta)*, 'the [*numeral*] Augustan Cohort (*or* Ala) of Thracians': see *Britannia* 27 (1996) 449.

7   Several successive glass furnaces were recovered, together with a large quantity of waste glass droplets and moiles (snapped-off waste from vessel production), as well as cullet (broken glass collected for melting). Products included small glass bottles, faïence melon beads, rings, and twisted rods for mixing medicines and cosmetics.

8   Each weighed between 173 and 177 lb. Two bore the cast stamp *IMP VESPASIAN AVG*, the third was from a different mould, with the inscription *IMP VESPASIANI AVG*, both for *Imp(eratoris) Vespasiani(i) Aug(usti)*, 'Property of the Emperor Augustus'. On the side of each was the cast inscription *BRIT EX ARG VEB*, *(plumbum) Brit(annicum) ex arg(entariis) Veb(...)*, 'British lead from the Veb(...) silver works'. The suggested date was early in the reign (Hassall, supra n.6).

9   Most extensively discussed in P. Marsden, "The excavation of a Roman palace in London, 1961-1972," *TransLonMiddxArchSoc* 26 (1975) 1-102.

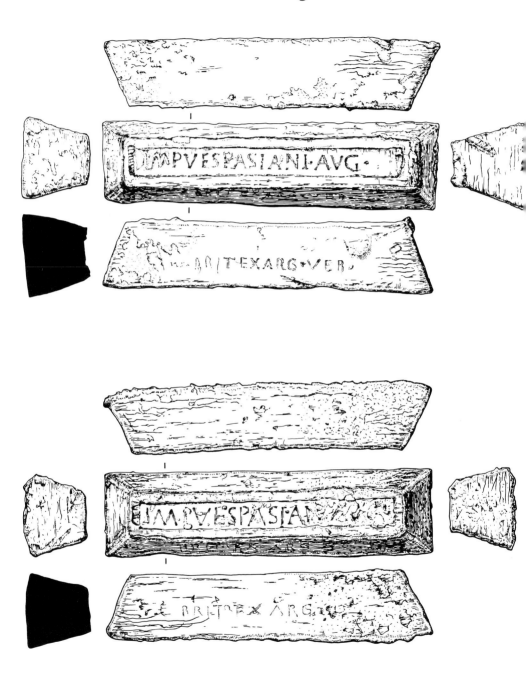

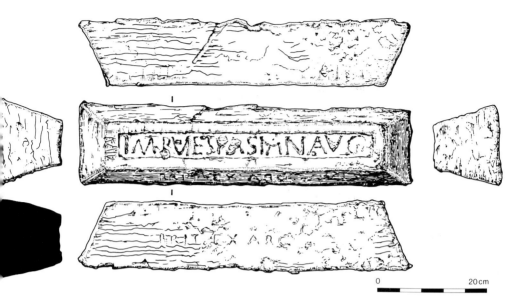

0   20 cm

Fig.6. The three lead ingots from Regis House. Stamped on the upper face of two of them was: IMP VESPASIAN AUG, and on the third IMP VESPASIANI AUG, denoting that they were the property of the Emperor Vespasian (69-79). All three bore additional stamps on the side: BRIT EX ARG VEB ('Britannia, from the silver mines'). The ingots are thought to have been produced at the Mendip mines in SW England.

contained massive walls which may have been the base of an imposing tower room, it was confined to the upper terraces.

In the 120s, the whole waterfront downstream of the Walbrook was rebuilt on a line considerably further out into the river.[10] Existing buildings and properties were extended to take advantage of the reclaimed land. Renovations were made to the warehouses at Regis House and the supposed palace, where new wings enclosed a courtyard

---

10   There were some localised alterations previous to this, including a substantial revetment built at Regis House in 102 to replace the Neronian quay, and a quay of similar date built at Pudding Lane to replace the earlier landing stage. The Hadrianic waterfront currently lies below the north side of the present dual-carriageway of Thames Street, and is largely inaccessible, although revetments of the period were recorded in the east at Billingsgate Buildings and at Suffolk House, where a structure built in 128 linked the two sections of late 1st-c. quay between the bridge and the Walbrook.

and a central pool. Other entirely new buildings were also erected, including a substantial townhouse next door to the supposed palace (fig. 2, site 28).[11]

Despite a widespread fire between 125 and 130, the waterfront continued to expand, and by about 140-60 had reached the south side of the present dual-carriageway of Thames Street (fig. 2).[12] Further advances took place about 180, by which time the waterfront included an isolated quay constructed at the Custom House site near the Tower of London (fig. 3, site 9).[13]

Around 200, great efforts were made to restore a unified river frontage by constructing substantial quays on a scale similar to those seen in the 1st c. The process began upstream of the Walbrook, proceeding eastward until by c.225 it had incorporated and extended beyond the quay at Custom House.[14] Contemporary timber-framed buildings were recorded at Swan Lane and Seal House (fig. 3, sites 19, 20). High-quality buildings were apparently restricted to an area well back from the waterfront and included townhouses near Billingsgate, Queen Street, and St Peter's Hill (fig. 3, site 16).

This great effort, however, presaged the decay of the port; between 250-70 the wharf was dismantled to or below the high-water mark (OD). There is no known historical event to explain this destructive

---

11 Originally recorded in the 1960s (Marsden [supra n.9]), this important structure has recently been investigated at Suffolk House.
12 Represented by revetments constructed downstream of the bridge at Custom House (fig. 2, site 7: 1973), New Fresh Wharf (fig. 2, site 19: 1974-78), and upstream by quays at Seal House (fig. 2, site 25: 1974) and Swan Lane (fig. 2, site 29: 1982). Thames Street, parallel to the north bank of the river, was the riparian road in the early mediaeval period, broadly following the line of the late Roman riverside wall. Later mediaeval reclamation south of Thames Street has left the present road some distance from the river. It has been a dual-carriageway since the 1960s.
13 Revetments are recorded at New Fresh Wharf, Seal House and Swan Lane (fig. 3, sites 15, 19, 20). The Custom House quay was unusually well built, using contiguous beams to create three rows of rigid self-supporting boxes; this form of construction was shared with contemporary quays built on the E bank of the Walbrook at Cannon Street Station (fig. 3, site 6) and possibly in the mouth of the Walbrook at Dowgate Hill House (fig. 3, site 10: 1986).
14 Sites upstream of the bridge include Bull Wharf (fig. 3, site 5: 1991, 1996), Vintry House (fig. 3, site 25: 1989, 1991), Thames Exchange (fig. 3, site 21: 1988), Swan Lane, and Seal House. Sites downstream include New Fresh Wharf, Billingsgate Lorry Park (fig. 3, site 4: 1982-83), and Custom House.

act; the decline of the town and its international trade may have led to the shrinkage of the port. The process was already complete when the construction after 270 of a riverside defensive wall severed town from river, and prevented any attempts at revival.[15]

The waterfront in Southwark

The suburb on the south bank consisted of a series of sand and gravel islands shaped by the river and regularly subject to flooding. The bridgehead would have required protection from the time of its construction, although there is no evidence for this before c.70-80, at which period revetted embankments have been recorded on either side of the bridgehead.[16] Although there were no substantial quays to match the wharves of the north bank, the construction of revetments permitted progressive reclamation of the main island west of the bridge in the late 1st and mid 2nd c., allowing buildings to extend across the tidal flats. These structures included a timber warehouse dated to 152 at Courage's Brewery (fig. 2, site 6)[17] and a massive masonry building, possibly with an official function, at Winchester Palace (fig. 2, site 33: see Westman below, and Yule and Rankov). Around 160, the E side of the main island was reclaimed behind a front-braced revetment, a length of which was recorded at Guy's Hospital.

There is little further evidence for later waterfront activity in Southwark, although maintenance was clearly carried out to protect the low-lying fringes of the suburb against incursions by the river.

---

15 Discussed at length in C. Hill, M. Millett and T. Blagg, *The Roman riverside wall and monumental arch in London, 1974-76* (London & Middx Arch. Soc. Special Paper 3, 1980). The riverside wall has been found on several sites, most recently next to the Tower of London at Three Quays House (fig. 3, site 22: 1996). The wall was built directly on top of the mid 2nd-c. revetment for virtually its entire length, and the Walbrook was probably divided into two smaller channels and diverted through it.

16 At the sites of Toppings Wharf (1974) and Winchester Palace (1983), both the subjects of publications in preparation.

17 A discussion of this well-preserved building has recently been published by T. Brigham, D. Goodburn *et al.*, "A Roman timber building on the Southwark waterfront, London," *ArchJ* 152 (1995) 1-72. The structure was probably privately owned. Entirely of timber, the floor level was 0.7 m below the contemporary ground level, and within the tidal range, suggesting that it was used for storage of goods, such as imported oils and wines, which required cool, damp conditions.

Construction techniques on the waterfront

The quays on the north bank show a clear structural development through the Roman period, although it should be stressed that many of the 2nd-c. structures on the waterfront were post-and-plank revetments, rather than quays. Space does not permit a detailed discussion of carpentry techniques, but there was a move towards the use of smaller timbers. The baulks used in the quay-front, for example, were reduced from scantlings on average 0.50 m in A.D. 63 to 0.30 m on average in 225. There were also structural changes to reduce the number of baulks required by the increased use of anchor piles to retain tiebacks in place of the original rear wall (fig. 4: compare examples of late 1st-c. and late 2nd/early 3rd-c. quays).

This more economic use of timber[18] was matched by a development in the use of joints. The 1st-c. use of lap joints to attach tiebacks to the quay-front was replaced from the mid 2nd c. by hidden dovetail joints, a more elegant solution which would allow vessels to moor directly alongside. An innovation of *c*.200 was the adoption of supporting piles driven into the foreshore under the frontage of the quay and mortised to the underside of the base timber to prevent the whole structure from slipping or sinking. Later quays constructed downstream of the bridge rested on beams laid on the foreshore and lapped under the base timber. Small free tenons — squared pieces of timber mortised into the adjoining faces at each level — were also introduced to hold the various tiers of quay frontage together.

The production of timber for these massive quays and contemporary revetments shows a considerable level of expertise in the exploitation of woodlands, and this is visible in other structures as well, including the warehouse at Courage's Brewery. Many timbers were cut to fairly standard sizes; it is clear, for example, that oak baulks were trimmed to 1.0 and 1.5 Roman ft (0.296 and 0.44 m) and used either whole or sawn into planks.

The port as a facility

Despite the scope of the area investigated, the buildings at Regis

---

18   It is not clear why the Romans did not embrace the use of post-and-plank revetments as an alternative to quay structures. A study of Roman and mediaeval revetments of similar design demonstrates that their lifespan from construction to replacement was comparable to that of quays, so a considerable saving in timber could have been made.

House (fig. 2, site 24; fig. 5) and Pudding Lane/Peninsular House (fig. 2, sites 22, 23) remain the only structures which can be identified with any confidence as public warehouses, and even there glass-making and other uses were discernible. There were undoubtedly public warehouses, granaries, and markets, including the great forum, scattered through the town away from the waterfront. Private stores, such as that at Courage's Brewery (fig. 2, site 6; fig. 13 below), together with merchants' premises and shops — indistinguishable from private houses — would have substantially augmented these facilities. This explains the high level of trade suggested by the volume of imported pottery, glassware and other products. The goods could have been handled without the need for the massive storehouses of the kind seen at Ostia, Carthage, Lepcis Magna, and Rome. This model of the port implies that cargo handling took place not simply at specific points near buildings dedicated for storage, but along the full length of the wharf.[19] We can picture small boats busily unloading sea-going vessels moored midstream, with local vessels and coasters beached on the foreshore.[20]

Sea-level change: a Roman tidal regression[21]

The first part of this paper discussed extensions of the waterfront made on average every 30 years, that had reclaimed up to 50 m of land from the river in the area of the central bridgehead by the end of the period. The reason for this continual expansion appears to have been a substantial and progressive fall in river level of 1.5 m between c.50 and 250, with the level of the wharf itself dropping from 2.0 m OD to 0.5 m OD over the same period. The foundation level of the riverside wall showed the level continued to fall after 270, although by the late Saxon period the river had regained and begun to surpass its former

---

19   Throughout the period, the wharf appears to have been deliberately maintained as an open space rarely less than 4.0 m wide. It should perhaps be seen not simply as a wharf but as a public riparian thoroughfare, no different in purpose from any of the town's main streets.

20   Boats of the Roman period found in London include a river craft of the mid 2nd c. found near Blackfriars (1962), a sea-going trader of the mid 3rd c. found at County Hall (1910), and a possible river lighter of the late 2nd c. from New Guy's House (1958). They have been discussed in a recent work by P. Marsden, *Ships of the port of London: first to eleventh centuries A.D.* (English Heritage 1994). A timber identified as the base of a dugout canoe was found next to a possible crane base in the 3rd-c. quay at Billingsgate Lorry Park (1983).

21   This subject has been discussed more fully in Brigham (supra n.1).

range. There have been several similar episodes since the last Ice Age, possibly caused by cycles of warming and cooling. The Roman episode is thought to have been the fifth and, to date, final episode of sea-level regression, represented elsewhere in Britain by peat growth on sea and river margins.[22] Without this regression, it is likely that the development of London's waterfront in the Roman period would have been rather different, with the timber quays being replaced by a more permanent masonry wharf. Against a backdrop of decline in the economy of the northern provinces, which served to make large-scale facilities redundant, the fall in river levels may have contributed to the final abandonment of the port.

---

22   The classic study of this regression is R. Devoy, "Flandrian sea-level changes and vegetational history of the Lower Thames Estuary," *Philosophical Transactions of the Royal Society of London* B 285 (1979) 355-407. Devoy recognised six phases of sea-level rise (transgression) since the last glaciation (10,000 BP). The phases of transgression (Thames I-VI) were punctuated by five phases of regression (Tilbury I-V). The regressive interludes were recognised in the depositional sequence as bands of peats, other organic material and raised beaches, and could be dated using radiocarbon analysis. One regressive phase (Tilbury V) dated to the Roman period. The sequence of firmly dated quays in London and the levels of their contemporary foreshores agree with Devoy's earlier explanation.

The development of the town plan of early Roman London

Peter Rowsome

This paper considers aspects of the planned development of Roman London during the town's first few decades — a period of near continuous construction and growth, from the town's foundation in c. A.D. 50 up until the time of its greatest commercial prosperity in the early 2nd c.[1] Over the past 20 years archaeological investigation of redevelopment sites in the heart of the Roman town has recorded complex stratigraphic sequences which reveal the topographic development of the early town, especially the street-system and private buildings. Detailed topographical data has provided an insight into the character and status of Roman London that complements the knowledge gained from the investigation of public buildings.[2]

Strategic and economic factors favoured London's location on the Thames. The area had not been the site of Iron Age native settlement, but in the changed circumstances of lowland Britain after the Roman conquest London was perfectly situated to become the economic centre of the new province, its position on the Thames ensuring that it would be both the major port and the focus of the road-system. The earliest Roman development would have followed the establishment of the river-crossing[3] at the lowest bridgeable point on the Thames, a point also suitable for port facilities. The crossing was associated with construction of that part of Roman Watling Street which crossed tidal mudflats south of the river, while north of the Thames it made a T-junction on Cornhill with an E-W route which led west towards Calleva (Silchester) and Verulamium (St Albans).

The plan of Roman London, like town plans throughout the western Roman empire, was clearly regulated. Its early streets were associated with the construction of road-side residential and commercial buildings characteristic of a quickly expanding, timber-built settlement. Beyond the area of the forum on the eastern hill, the street pattern was order-

---

1   See D. Perring, *Roman London* (London 1991) esp. 1-75 for an account of London's early growth.

2   The papers by Bateman and Brigham in this volume look at *Londinium*'s public buildings and waterfront installations respectively.

3   Perhaps initially a rope-ferry, it was replaced by a timber bridge at an early date; see Brigham above.

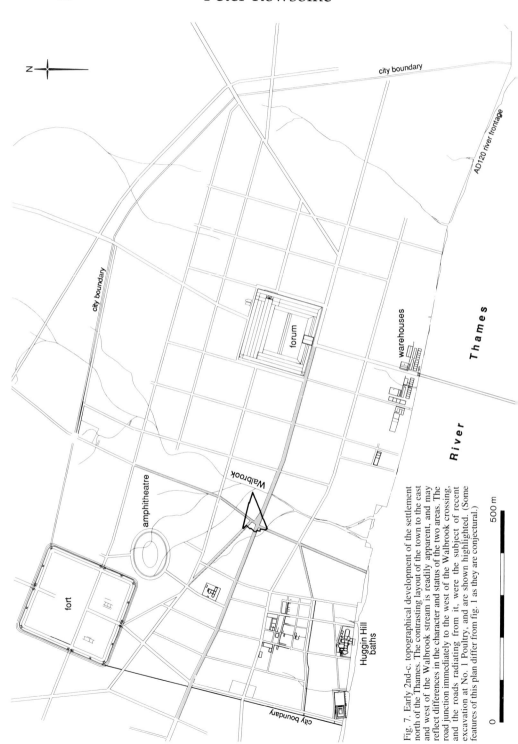

Fig. 7. Early 2nd-c. topographical development of the settlement north of the Thames. The contrasting layout of the town to the east and west of the Walbrook stream is readily apparent, and may reflect differences in the character and status of the two areas. The road junction immediately to the west of the Walbrook crossing, and the roads radiating from it, were the subject of recent excavation at No. 1 Poultry, and are shown highlighted. (Some features of this plan differ from fig. 1 as they are conjectural.)

city boundary

AD120 river frontage

city boundary

forum

warehouses

Thames

River

amphitheatre

Walbrook

fort

Huggin Hill baths

city boundary

0   500 m

ed, though not rigidly orthogonal.[4] Much of the Neronian and Flavian–
Trajanic growth appears to have taken place in an organic manner but
sufficiently controlled to ensure that all parts of the town were
planned.[5] With the exception of the Boudiccan destruction of London in
60-61 and its aftermath, the town experienced strong growth throughout the 1st c. The vigorous growth of the Flavian city was characterized not only by a major public building programme but also by the
expansion of the street system and by much private building within the
boundaries of the settlement (fig. 7).[6] Once established, the street
pattern and the property boundaries of road-side buildings showed a
high degree of stability, unaffected by incidents such as fires or
pronounced social and economic changes over time.

A study of the town's planned development may also shed light on
its character, status, and inhabitants.[7] London was not a *civitas* capital
and may not have gained an official status until quite late, if ever. The
earliest historical record of London describes it on the eve of the
Boudiccan revolt as 'not distinguished by the title of colony yet
exceedingly famous for its wealth of traders and commercial traffic'.[8]
The suggestion that it may have been an unofficial but planned trading

---

4   A relatively small area on Cornhill, on the location of the later forum and
      basilica, may have been the site of the very first settlement, although no
      boundaries to it have been positively identified; see Perring (supra n.1). It is
      also important to note that London's town plan had as its focus an open
      public space on the site of the Flavian forum; see D. Perring, "Spatial
      organisation and social change in Roman towns," in J. Rich and A. Wallace-
      Hadrill (edd.), *City and country in the ancient world* (London 1991).

5   Radial or strip-development spread westwards along the main E-W road
      from a very early date, but close examination indicates that the road-side
      development was ordered. See the case study of the excavations at No. 1
      Poultry on the following pages.

6   Evidence of the boundaries of the enlarged settlement, the street grid, and the
      early Flavian public building programme indicates that many of the major
      public buildings, such as the Huggin Hill Public Baths and a nearby temple,
      were in peripheral locations. This may indicate that major public amenities
      were intended to form separate foci for the urban area. It may be related to
      the idea of urban armatures — public facilities interconnected by public
      open space — discussed by W. L. MacDonald, *The architecture of the Roman
      Empire* II: *an urban appraisal* (New Haven 1986).

7   The study of Roman London has tremendous potential in this regard as the
      town has been the subject of more detailed archaeological investigation than
      most others in the western empire.

8   Tac., *Ann.* 14.33.

settlement of Roman citizens, a *conventus civium Romanorum*, may help explain the town's dramatic early growth.[9] Its openness may have offered settlers not only economic opportunities but also opportunities for social advancement.[10] But there seems little doubt that London had official sanction from the outset: it may have been deliberately created to serve as an entrepôt for the new province.[11] In this case, a public official may have had a say in the development of the town and public investment in it.[12]

London was effectively divided into three parts by the Walbrook stream and the Thames.[13] The developed street systems and the type and variety of buildings differed markedly in different parts of the town, and this seems to have been more than simply a consequence of variations in the natural topography. In the eastern and western parts of the town the street-systems were quite dissimilar (fig. 7). It has been argued that these differences may reflect the fact that the three areas were of different status, the eastern hill perhaps being the *conventus civium Romanorum*, the western hill partly a military settlement, and the area south of the river a community of non-citizens.[14] It would seem a reasonable proposition that communities housing residents of different status would differ in their topographical development.

---

9   J. Morris, *Londinium – London in the Roman empire* (London 1982) 104. The view is developed by J. J. Wilkes, "The status of Londinium," in *Interpreting London* 27-31.

10   The absence of a pre-Roman tribal élite may have removed social barriers to the advancement of settlers. See T. Williams, "The foundation and early development of Roman London: a social context," *Antiquity* 64 (1990) 599-607.

11   M. Millett, "Characterizing Roman London," in *Interpreting London* 33-37.

12   London's administrative status remains unclear. While both the imperial procurator and consular legate may have been resident at London even prior to the Boudiccan revolt, the administrative capital may have remained at Camulodunum (Colchester) until some time later; see P. Salway, *Roman Britain* (Oxford 1981) and M. Hassall, "London as a provincial capital," in *Interpreting London* 19-26.

13   The significance of the Thames and the Walbrook as boundaries may be connected with their possible religious aspect. In the case of the Walbrook, there is disagreement as to whether metal finds from deposits within the stream were votive or simply lost objects; see R. Merrifield, *Roman London* (London 1969) esp. 168-203, for an argument in favour of the Walbrook as a sacred stream, and T. Wilmott, *Excavations in the Middle Walbrook valley* (London & Middx Arch. Soc. Special Paper 13, 1991) for an alternative view.

14   See M. Millett, "Evaluating Roman London," *ArchJ* 151 (1994) 427-34, and Millett above.

The large amount of archaeological evidence relating to London's planned development[15] cannot be summarised in detail here, but aspects of the settlement's topographical and social character can be illustrated through a look at the section immediately west of the Walbrook stream, an area which has recently been the subject of extensive excavation.[16]

1st-c. planned development at Poultry

The pre-Roman topography of the area was dominated by a natural slope down to the Walbrook, with less pronounced slopes along tributaries; they delineated a raised, gravel plateau which protruded into the valley. The *via decumana*, the primary E-W road through the settlement from Cornhill, crossed the area; its location corresponded with the gravel ridge, which provided the most convenient point to bridge the Walbrook and then continue west to cross the Fleet.

Extensive landscaping and drainage work took place at the same time that the main road was constructed. A relatively narrow, poorly-metalled gravel track provided a temporary access. The primary metalling of the main road was formed of rammed gravel laid on a raised road-bed of sand and clay-silt. The road, initially *c.*7.5 m wide, later widened to 9 m, was flanked by timber box drains, which carried surface water east to the Walbrook. To the north-east of the road, a series of flat terraces were cut into the prevailing natural slope, while to the south of the road timber structures backfilled with midden layers were used to consolidate a wet area prior to its development. The Walbrook itself was straightened and canalized.[17] Shortly after

---

15   The antiquarian evidence is summarised in the gazetteer section of R. Merrifield, *The Roman city of London* (London 1965). See D. Perring (supra n.1) for an updated review of the evidence.

16   Between April 1994 and June 1996, the Museum of London Archaeology Service undertook the controlled archaeological excavation of 3,400 m^2 at No. 1 Poultry, London EC4. A programme of analysis and publication, funded by English Heritage, is underway. Interim reports on the excavations include P. Rowsome, "Number 1 Poultry — evaluation and Phase 1 excavations," *London Archaeologist* 7.14 (1995) 371-82, and M. Burch *et al.*, "Number 1 Poultry — the main excavation: Roman sequence," *London Archaeologist* 8.5 (1997) 127-36. A summary appears in "Roman Britain in 1996: sites explored," *Britannia* (1997).

17   The earliest evidence of modification to the W bank of the Walbrook was a

Fig. 8. Part of a narrow pre-Boudiccan road ran NW from the street junction discovered at No. 1 Poultry. The road, which remained in use until the 4th c., was constructed from layers of highly compacted gravel to form successive road surfaces, and is typical of Roman roads within *Londinium*.

the construction of the main road, a road junction was offset on the higher ground of the western part of the site, with roads leading NW (fig. 8) towards the area of the later fort and amphitheatre[18] and

---

timber revetment between two terrace levels, dated dendrochronologically to 52-55. This is comparable in date to the Claudian pile-and-plank revetment from Regis House, dated dendrochronologically to 52, and is the earliest securely dated structure from Roman London. See T. Brigham *et al.*, "Current archaeological work at Regis House part 1," *London Archaeologist* 8.2 (1996) 33-34.

18   This important radial street leading NW from the Walbrook crossing is discussed in J. Shepherd and P. Rowsome, "The pre-urban and Roman topography in the King Street and Cheapside areas of the City of London," *TransLonMiddxArchSoc* 38 (1987) 11-58. It is of interest that the road leads

possibly also north towards the upper Walbrook.[19] These secondary roads, together with the *via decumana*, may have been part of the primary settlement of the area west of the Walbrook; they may have formed the principal junction before A.D. 60 in an area which was subject to planned development.[20] The construction of the roads heralded the opening of the area west of the Walbrook by delineating zones and *insulae* and by providing access to the boundaries of the settlement.

By 60-61, earth and timber buildings had been constructed along the road-sides to the west of the Walbrook crossing; the terracing of the site provided level plots for private building. The greatest concentration of road-side building lay on the higher ground to the north and west of the road junction. A larger portion of the lower, eastern terraces near the Walbrook remained open space crossed by timber-lined water channels and perhaps had already been set aside for industrial use.

Flavian expansion of the planned town

The removal of débris and the re-opening of the main roads and fac-

---

towards the site of the later fort and amphitheatre, where no evidence of pre-Flavian activity has been found. The first amphitheatre, which has been the subject of extensive controlled excavation, was built of timber and has been dated dendrochronologically to shortly after 70: see N. Bateman, "The London amphitheatre: excavations 1987-96," *Britannia* 1997. The masonry fort at Cripplegate has been dated to the early 2nd c.: see W. F. Grimes, *The excavation of Roman and mediaeval London* (London 1968) 17-40. The existence of a timber antecedent to the fort is thought possible (Perring [supra n.1] 39-40), and recent excavations at 3-9 Noble Street have found evidence of extensive Flavian occupation on the site of the later fort, although it was not clear that this was military.

19   The road north from Poultry may post-date the Boudiccan rebellion, and can be related to parts of a N-S aligned road along the W side of the Walbrook, leading to a primarily industrial area in the N part of the town; see C. Maloney, *The upper Walbrook in the Roman period* (CBA Res. Rep. 69, 1990) 26-77.

20   Some have argued that the very early settlement west of the Walbrook was a suburb of the planned core, and not incorporated into the formal town until *c*.70 or later: see, for instance, T. Williams, *Public buildings in the south-west quarter of Roman London* (CBA Res. Rep. 88, 1993) 33-38. Others contend that a large part of the western hill was identified from the outset as lying within the settlement: see D. Perring, S. Roskams, and P. Allen, *Early development of Roman London west of the Walbrook* (CBA Res. Rep. 70, 1991) 108-17, and Perring (supra n.1) 6-21. The evidence of extensive Neronian development at Poultry seems to support the latter view.

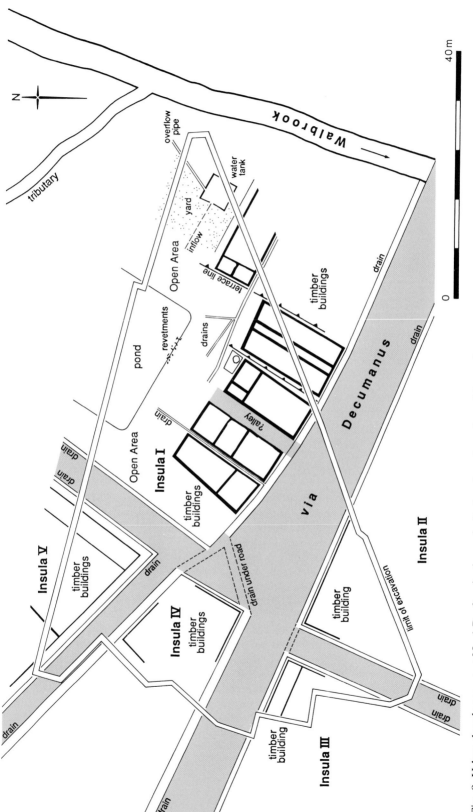

Fig. 9. Urban development at No 1 Poultry in the early 2nd c., based on the evidence from recent excavations there. Flavian–Trajanic expansion of the street system was associated with the construction of road-side buildings set closely together and with the creation of an industrial area in the northern part of Insula I and along the west bank of the Walbrook stream.

ilities must have taken priority in the years shortly after the Boudiccan rebellion. Evidence from Poultry and elsewhere indicates that
this was not accompanied by the rebuilding of road-side properties,
which at first were merely levelled and re-terraced.[21] The site of one
early building, on the south side of the main road opposite the pre-
Boudican junction, was not only cleared but replaced by a new road
aligned N–S to create a proper cross-roads (fig. 9).[22]

Parts of five Flavian *insulae* lay within the excavation's study
area, each containing successive phases of road-side timber buildings of
Flavian–Trajanic date (*c*.70-120). The new buildings displayed a greater variety of materials and styles of construction than did their predecessors,[23] and were set more closely together than before, particularly
in Insula I, but generally they reflected the alignments and plot boundaries of the buildings they replaced. In Insula I, parts of at least 5
road-side properties of mixed commercial and residential use were
built along the N side of the *via decumana*, each between 6 and 8 m in
width and *c*.16 m deep, and generally contained small room areas (*c*.3-4
m square). The buildings were bounded to the north by well-drained
back yards which may have contained small-scale industries operated
by the road-side residents (fig. 10).

The land further to the north in Insula I and extending east to the
Walbrook was developed as an industrial zone, part of which was occupied by a large feature tentatively identified as a pond or low area
prone to flooding. An oak-planked water-tank with clay lining to the
east (fig. 11) may have supplied water to a nearby trade or industry. It
was enclosed by a yard surfaced with broken and discarded fragments
of rotary quernstones.[24] Wear patterns indicate that the querns had
seen use, perhaps in a mill or bakery nearby, although it is also possible

---

21 Military or public facilities may have been rebuilt immediately after the
    rebellion. A new quayside in the port area was in place by 63 and new
    bridges over the Thames and the Walbrook may also have been a priority
    (see Brigham [supra n.18]). In contrast, it may have been some time before
    private individuals had the means or confidence to rebuild.

22 The road running north may also date from this time (supra n.20).

23 The majority of the late 1st-c. buildings recorded at Poultry had oak-pile
    foundations. Superstructures included forms with timber ground-beams and
    wall studs with wattle-and-daub infill, brickearth sills, mudbrick, and lathe
    and plaster. See Perring and Roskams (supra n.21) 67-107 for a review of
    building types found in early Roman London.

24 Over 1100 quern fragments were recovered from the area, the majority being
    a type of lava imported from the Mayen–Niedermendig region of Germany.

Peter Rowsome

Fig. 10. A large box-structure, made of oak beams, whose felling has been dendrochronologically dated to a range of A.D. 73 to 90, was constructed on the second terrace in insula 1 at No. 1 Poultry as a platform for road-side buildings. (Scale is 1 m long.) (MoLAS).

Fig. 11. A late 1st-c. water-tank located in what may have been an industrial area along the W bank of the Walbrook stream, No. 1 Poultry (MoLAS).

that they arrived in London as ballast after use elsewhere. The extent of the industrial activity and systems for managing water in the north part of Insula I suggests that it may have functioned independently from the road-side buildings to the south. These activities seem to have ended around the time of the Hadrianic fire of c.125.[25]

Conclusions

At London, as elsewhere in the empire, the Romans put concepts of the planned city into practice. This can be seen in the carefully planned siting and layout of the early town and in the provision of public works. Even in those decades which experienced the most rapid growth, there is little or no indication of unsanctioned development. The evidence from Poultry indicates that the primary street-system for the area west of the Walbrook was put in place at an early date and that it foreshadowed, and perhaps dictated, the positioning of later public buildings such as the Huggin Hill baths and the amphitheatre. Even the inclusion of open space within the boundaries of the early settlement at London should probably be seen as evidence of planning, since open space might confer prestige while at the same time providing scope for future planned development.

Acknowledgements

I would like to thank David Bentley of MoLAS for permission to use the map of the town plan of early Roman London based on his many years of work on the subject. The plan showing early Roman land-use at No. 1 Poultry was drawn by Susan Banks. Thanks also go to Martin Millett for his comments on the character and status of Roman London.

---

25 A large part of the town was destroyed by a fire in c.120-25, and rebuilding after the fire was generally less vigorous, the decline perhaps exacerbated by an economic contraction felt throughout the empire. London's commercial prospects, heavily reliant on its position as a centre of trade, must have suffered greatly from the economic and financial problems of the 2nd c. Shopkeepers and craftsmen may have left in large numbers, and city revenue may have declined owing to the loss of income from rents and customs: see Perring (supra n.1) 89.

Public buildings in Roman London: some contrasts

N. C. W. Bateman

Today in W Europe the distinction between 'private' and 'public' building might seem quite straightforward, but this does not mean that such modern concepts can be readily applied to the Roman period.[1] One definition which might appear useful is based upon the funding of the construction — but Roman conceptions of private and public expense were very different from our own. Another possible definition centres on use: to what degree is a building open to all, or not? But this is often hard to distinguish in the archaeological record, and some buildings, such as bath-houses in Roman London, are particularly susceptible to either interpretation.[2] Furthermore, it is very easy to confuse 'public' with 'monumental': *Londinium*'s waterfronts were public buildings in some sense, as were several free-standing structures tentatively identified as roadside screens or colonnades,[3] but none of these would normally appear in a catalogue of 'public buildings'.

This paper does not attempt to answer these wider issues of defini-

---

1   There is no real definition in ancient sources. Vitruvius was aware of the two categories and used them as a means of grouping, rather than defining, the buildings he discussed. Building, he said, can be divided into two parts, the first of which is private (*privatorum aedificiorum explicatio*). He added (1.3.1): "Now the assignment of public buildings [*publicorum*] is threefold: one, to defence; the second, to religion; the third, to convenience. The method of defence by walls, towers and gates has been devised with a view to the continuous warding off of hostile attacks; to religion belongs the planning of the shrines and sacred temples of the immortal gods; to convenience, the disposal of public sites for the general use, such as harbours, opens spaces, colonnades, baths, theatres, promenades, and other things which are planned, with like purposes, in public situations."

2   Cf. Perring's remarks on the interpretation of the Pudding Lane bath-house (fig. 2, site 23) as part of a (public) inn or a private house (D. Perring, *Roman London* [London 1991] 73). Note also that the 3rd-c. mithraeum (fig. 3, site 27) was probably attached to a private house (ibid. 105).

3   Excavations in Bishopsgate in 1993 (fig. 2, site 13) and Borough High St., Southwark (fig. 2, site 15) in 1995 (unpublished). Compare also the structure at Gateway House (fig. 2, site 11) in J. Shepherd, "The Roman features at Gateway House and Watling House, Watling Street, City of London 1954," *TransLonMiddxArchSoc* 38 (1987) 11-58, fig. 11.

tion. However, by contrasting a few of London's larger buildings, which at least were clearly intended to impress, it is possible to identify certain themes that underscore the need for further work on 'public buildings'.

The Huggin Hill bath-house (fig. 2, site 8) is the kind of structure generally accepted as a public building. Recent work has shown that considerable attention was paid to preparation of the site: the ground was consolidated with extensive oak piling and a concrete raft 1 m thick formed a platform for the superstructure.[4] Primary construction probably occurred around 75-80. Although not massive by continental standards, the baths were among the largest in Britain. The sophistication and precision of the design indicates a military surveyor, and the transport of material up the Thames, as well as much of the labour necessary for construction, may also have been provided by the military. Nevertheless, these were probably civilian, not military baths.[5]

A significant enlargement of the building in the early 2nd c. may have been associated with Hadrian's visit in 122. However, shortly after c.140 the baths were abandoned.[6] Walls were razed and, after careful removal of mosaics, marble and other embellishments, rooms were deliberately filled with rubble. This organised demolition was

---

4   The complex was first identified in 1964 and recent large-scale excavations took place in 1988-89. I am indebted to P. Rowsome, director of the excavations, for much of the information which follows. See also his "The Huggin Hill Baths and other bath buildings in Roman London — barometers of the town's changing circumstances?," in a JRA Supplement, forthcoming.

5   It has been suggested that there was a similar civilian institution on the eastern hill, possibly in the area of the so-called 'Governor's Palace' (fig. 2, site 4). Excavations here between 1961 and 1972 revealed mosaics, *opus signinum* floors, substantial walls, hypocausts, and large basins lined with *opus signinum*. Initial interpretation favoured the idea of a single large private residence (P. Marsden, "The excavation of a Roman palace site in London, 1961-1972," *TransLonMiddxArchSoc* 26 [1975] 1-102; and ibid. 29 [1978] 99-103). However, recent work at the Cannon Street site (1988-89) makes it clear that this is not one building of (nearly) symmetrical design but a palimpsest of several different buildings. At least some of them are likely to have been public buildings, and there may have been a public bath (G. Milne, *Roman London* [London 1995] 91-93; Perring [supra n.2] 30-33; G. Milne, "A palace disproved: reassessing the provincial governor's presence in 1st-century London," in *Interpreting London* 49-55.

6   Milne (*Roman London* ibid. 87) has pointed out that, although there are several 4th-c. private bath-houses, no public baths have been found which might have served the town in the 3rd c.

not necessitated by serious structural flaws, nor was the land subsequently abandoned; clay and timber buildings which lasted to *c*.300 utilised the terrace revetment which had formed the precinct wall for the baths, and some form of property continuity has been suggested.

One of the earliest of the monumental buildings in the southwest part of *Londinium* has been convincingly reconstructed as a large temple complex in the classical style (fig. 2, site 35), similar in size and layout to the Temple of Sulis Minerva at Bath,[7] although its dedication is unknown. The entrance to the precinct faced east; at a later stage, the entrance may have been a monumental arch (fig. 3, site 30), a reconstruction of which is based upon decorated stones found in the riverside defensive wall.[8] It was flanked by a monumental façade along the river. Substantial ashlar blocks and decorative elements found re-used in later buildings suggest that the temple was large, well-built, and impressive.[9] There is little dating evidence for the temple's construction, though its demolition to make way for the Allectan palace complex (fig. 3, site 16) can be dated to before 293-94.[10] The precinct

---

7   I am grateful to D. Bentley of MoLAS for an explanation of his work of reconstructing this temple. Preliminary assessment of the evidence was given in T. Williams, *Public buildings in the south-west quarter of Roman London* (CBA Res. Rep. 88, 1993). The temple appears to be laid out on an alignment that is not only quite different to that of the later Allectan palace complex, but also to that of the contemporary waterfront. This is significant in view of recent assertions of the importance of the Thames frontage in establishing monumental buildings (T. Blagg, "Monumental architecture in Roman London," in *Interpreting London* 43-47, esp. 45). It is noticeable that the central axis of the temple, if extrapolated eastwards, pointed directly at the front of the forum.

8   T. Blagg, "The sculptured stones," in C. Hill, M. Millett and T. Blagg, *The Roman riverside wall and monumental arch in London* (London & Middx Arch. Soc. Special Paper 3, 1980) 125-83. The arch is dated to the Antonine period or later. Other re-used stones imply the existence of a so-called 'Screen of the Gods'. There is a possibility that both structures were constructed in the late 2nd c. and related to the visit of the emperor Septimius Severus (Perring [supra n.2] 93-95).

9   This paper will not consider the issue of whether *Londinium* had a temple to the cult of the emperor (cf. Perring [supra n.2] 34), but it is unlikely that this temple served that purpose since such temples are usually close to the forum (e.g., at Colchester, Lyon, and Tarragona).

10   Dendrochronology has provided accurate dating for the construction of the new building, which has allowed an association with known historical events: see Williams (supra n.7). However, Blagg (supra n.7, 46) has pointed

wall lies just within the Flavian town boundary immediately to the west. The complex occupied one of three nearly equal blocks laid out along the W waterfront (fig. 2 at A, B and C). This pattern may suggest that it formed part of an official division of land for large (monumental?) 'public buildings' in the Flavian period.[11]

Recent excavations have revealed much new information about the second forum, which was built between 100 and 120-30.[12] The complex was massive, measuring *c*.165 by 165 m, and the basilica was probably the largest Roman building north of the Alps.[13] Nevertheless, the complex seems to have been seriously flawed, since many of the foundation trenches were dug and then allowed to fill with organic waste before the foundations were built. As it decayed this waste compacted, causing much subsidence and cracking. Many floors, including that of the nave of the basilica, were laid over hastily backfilled quarry-pits,

---

out that the temple should already have been abandoned for it to have been demolished without risking accusations of impiety.

11   This has sometimes been used to justify the suggestion of specific 'zones' within *Londinium* for commerce, industry, and 'public buildings'. Yet there is little real evidence that the Romans utilized such rigid planning. More probably this was a strip of available and recently cleared or reclaimed land.

12   Excavations at Leadenhall Court (fig. 2, site 17) and Whittington Avenue (fig. 2, site 32) between 1984 and 1988. There were 13 other excavations over the forum between 1881 and 1977. See P. Marsden, *The Roman forum site in London: discoveries before 1985* (London 1987). I am indebted to T. Brigham for discussions about the forum: see also his "A reassessment of the second basilica in London, A.D. 100-400: excavations at Leadenhall Court 1984-86," *Britannia* 21 (1990) 53-97. These recent excavations did not encounter the smaller first forum complex (fig. 2, site 12) which was built in *c*.75 and measured *c*.100 by 50 m (Milne [supra n.5] 52-53). This early forum had an oblong shape that was characteristic of continental fora rather than British ones, although it lacked a temple at one end (Blagg [supra n.7] 43). Possibly associated with this first complex was the nearby Flavian aisled hall at Fenchurch Street excavated in 1983 (fig. 2, site 10). This hall was quite large (19 x *c*.11 m), with floors of *opus signinum* and fine painted plaster walls, and has been interpreted as a possible guild (*collegium*) hall. It seems to have been demolished by the time the second forum was built (Perring [supra n.2] 35).

13   In spite of its size, the complex has been described as rather utilitarian in some respects (Blagg [supra n.7] 44). There is no evidence that the construction of this building, or the earlier forum, accompanied any change of London's status, much less an elevation to *municipium* (M. Millett, "Evaluating Roman London," *ArchJ* 151 [1994] 427-34, esp. 432).

with similar results. That this was a contemporary problem is demon-strated by evidence for rebuilding and patching over many of the cracks, probably within a few decades of the original construction. Nevertheless, the forum remained in use until c.270-300, a period in which there is evidence of abandonment of at least parts of the build-ing.[14] At the beginning of the 4th c., the walls of the basilica and forum were razed to the ground and the area was left as a wide, empty space.[15] It is not obvious that the building was demolished for local redevelopment.[16]

There is now considerable evidence that the first amphitheatre (fig. 2) was built entirely in timber, probably shortly after c.70.[17] Most of this structure was removed to make way for a rebuilding, probably not long after 120, that made limited use of masonry for the arena and the walls of the entrances, although even these were probably only c.2.5 m high (fig. 12). The rest of the structure, including the whole cavea, continued to be built of timber. Although fairly large by British standards, the amphitheatre could not be described as monumental.[18] The rebuilding may have been associated with Hadrian's visit in c.122, since he was an enthusiast both for building and for gladiatorial

---

14   Silt deposits accumulated over many floors, and at least one room was choked with débris from a localised fire. Mud, marked with wheel ruts, accumulated over the road along the N side of the forum (Brigham, pers. comm.).

15   The director of the 1984 excavation, G. Milne (supra n.5, 81), placed great stress on how this demolition was "systematic and total, the entire superstructure razed to the ... ground".

16   However, Brigham suggests that there is a possibility that the southern range of the forum may have been left standing (pers. comm.).

17   London's amphitheatre was discovered in 1988 and excavation has been more or less continuous to 1996: see N. Bateman, "The London amphitheatre: excavations 1987-1996," Britannia 28 (1997). Dating cited here is provisional and largely derived from dendrochronology. No evidence of a separate theatre has been identified in London. Some have suggested the possibility of a circus precinct in the southwest part of the town (the Knightrider Street walls; see fig. 2, site 16) but the evidence is weak (Perring [supra n.2] 60).

18   The rebuilt amphitheatre must have been between 90 and 110 m in length and it may have held more than 7,000 spectators: see Bateman (supra n.17). The masonry walls comprised courses of tile and ragstone. The only stone elements identified were some threshold stones and two half-rounded coping stones from the top of the arena wall.

Fig.12. The curving arena wall of the amphitheatre. The E entrance, flanked by two side chambers, is on the right.

shows.[19] Such a date is similar to the conventional date for the military fort, which lay *c*.30 m to the northwest, and it seems reasonable to suggest that soldiers were employed in the re-building of the amphitheatre as well as the fort.[20] The presence of an earlier timber amphitheatre would lend weight to the suggestion of an earlier fort.[21] Notwithstanding their close proximity, however, even the timber amphitheatre seems too large to have catered to an exclusively military audience.[22] There is good reason to believe that the amphitheatre was still being used at least until the end of the 3rd c.[23] After abandonment in the early 4th c., most of the masonry walls were robbed, although coins from the robber fills indicate that this did not happen before 367.

Conclusions

The study of public buildings is probably the key to understanding the political power structure of a town.[24] British towns have fewer public buildings than continental ones, and there is little evidence for

---

19   Cass. Dio 69.10.1; *SHA*, Hadr. 14.11.

20   The fort was first recognised after World War II (W. Grimes, *The excavation of Roman and mediaeval London* [London 1968] 17-40). Recent suggestions are more cautious and suggest the period of 90-120 for construction (Milne [supra n.5] 59; Perring [supra n.2] 39-40).

21   The existence of an earlier fort has long been sought, either in this area or elsewhere (see summary in Perring [supra n.2] 40). No evidence for an early fort was found in the Shelley House excavations of 1996 (fig. 2, site 26), though there was nothing which disproved it. There was, however, evidence of extensive Flavian occupation in the area (D. Lakin, pers. comm.).

22   Recent estimates of the fort's complement have ranged from 1,000 to 2,000 men. It would have included parts of the governor's administrative staff and guard, men in transit, various groups in 'intelligence', and some responsible for prisoners: see Perring (supra n.2) 39-40; M. W. Hassall, "Roman soldiers in Roman London," in D. E. Strong (ed.), *Archaeological theory and practice* (1973) 231-37.

23   However, sheep and horse bones found in the highest deposits of the amphitheatre may represent late use of the amphitheatre as a market, and a change of function after its spectacular uses grew too expensive.

24   It is noticeable, for instance, that there is nothing which could be described as a 'public building' from the boom period before the Boudiccan revolt. The contrast with the period immediately following must be related to a change in the nature of the town's occupation, and in the way the inhabitants perceived their community.

the involvement of local élites in urban public building.[25] In continental Europe, competitive munificence was encouraged and became fundamental to the development of cities, but there is no good evidence for it in *Londinium*. This may be the result of the town's foundation as a new trading centre at the margins of existing social and political groups, rather than at a pre-existing tribal centre.[26]

The buildings discussed above are notable for the contrasts which they provide. Why were some buildings, like the temple and the baths, well built, whereas others, like the theoretically more important forum complex, were not? Why, in these circumstances, were the baths demolished in the mid 2nd c. while the forum survived to the 4th c.? Why were massive quantities of masonry and cut stone used for those buildings, yet the contemporary amphitheatre was built in timber and, even when rebuilt, remained inferior to amphitheatres at Chester and Caerleon, not to mention others in Europe?[27] Are there any implications to be drawn from the impression that there are more public buildings on the western hill than on the eastern?

If 'public buildings' in *Londinium* were not initiated by private citizens, were they 'officially' sponsored and if so by whom? There are three possible candidates for official sponsorship of public buildings. In Britannia, by far the greatest number of dedicatory inscriptions for such buildings comes from the military.[28] However, while some military involvement has been suggested for the Huggin Hill bath-house and

---

25   T. Blagg, "Architectural munificence in Britain: the evidence of inscrip tions," *Britannia* 21 (1990) 13-31; J. J. Wilkes, "Introduction," in P. E. Johnson (ed.), *Architecture in Roman Britain* (CBA Res. Rep. 94, 1996) 1-5. See also Blagg (supra n.7) 43. Wilkes, commenting on the Verulamium (A.D. 79) and Wroxeter (129) forum inscriptions, points out that both conceal more than they say. Although clearly carved by men expert in the correct forms of dedications, there is no mention of local people or, in particular, of local magistrates (Wilkes, ibid.). Millett points out that the passage which seems to indicate a specific policy of involving local élites in urban regeneration (Tac., *Agr.* 21) is the only such passage in ancient literature, and that it is frequently given too much weight (M. Millett, *The Romanization of Britain* [London 1990] 69).

26   Millett ibid. 89.

27   The conventional explanation — that amphitheatres never 'caught on' in Britain (with its implicit notion of relative cultural superiority) — seems inadequate in a town which must have been as cosmopolitan as any in the western empire.

28   Blagg (supra n.25).

indeed the amphitheatre, it is difficult to detect any military involvement in the forum.[29] A more likely 'official' sponsor might have been the office of the procurator.[30] A recent study of tiles stamped by the procurator's office shows that most have been found close to known public buildings: along the western waterfront, around the fort, amphitheatre, and forum, and in Southwark.[31] Another possible sponsor has been identified in the emperor.[32] The irregular and somewhat arbitrary nature of such sponsorship from outside might well explain the sporadic rate of construction of several public buildings. There was a remarkable burst of activity under two emperors in particular, Vespasian and Hadrian, both of whom visited the province.[33] However, there is little evidence that they formulated an over-arching 'policy' of urbanisation for this or any other province.

Perhaps the failure to find a definitive answer is the result in part of the atempt to distinguish a single sponsor.[34] The contrasts between different public buildings may actually reflect a variety of different agents, military, civil, local, and external. This may relate to an idea

---

29   Note also the 3rd-c. marble inscription by a military cohort involved with the public building at Winchester Palace (early 2nd to mid 4th-c.; see fig. 2, site 33), which has been interpreted as a military guild headquarters or *schola* (B. Yule, "Excavations at Winchester Palace, Southwark," *London Archaeologist* 6.2 [1989] 31-39; M. W. Hassall, "London as a provincial capital," in *Interpreting London* 19-26, esp. 23, and Yule and Rankov below). Note also that finds from excavations at the Regis House site in 1996 (fig. 2, site 24) suggest definite involvement of the military in the construction of the waterfront in 63 (B. Watson, pers. comm.).

30   Millett (supra n.25, 91) has suggested that the procurator moved to *Londinium* after the Boudiccan revolt, partly because of the advantages of a large town that was not tied to pre-existing tribal élites. The governor, on the other hand, was unlikely to have spent much time in the town.

31   I. M. Betts, "Procuratorial tile stamps from London," *Britannia* 26 (1995) 207-29. Doubts, however, have been raised about the degree to which such stamped tiles should be seen as evidence of state involvement in tile manufacture rather than in building construction (cf. Perring [supra n.2] 42; Blagg [supra n.7] 47).

32   P. Salway, *Roman Britain* (Oxford 1981); R. Merrifield, *London, city of the Romans* (London 1983) 87.

33   Vespasian visited Britannia before he was made emperor. Note, however, the suggestion of Septimius Severus's involvement in the public buildings of the SW quarter (supra n.8).

34   "It is difficult to form an overall picture of London's monumental architecture" (Blagg [supra n.7] 47).

which has recently received some attention, the notion of *Londinium* as dual (or plural) communities rather than a single entity. This theory identifies a possible military/official enclave on the western hill, and a civil *conventus civium Romanorum* on the eastern; it tends to side-step the debate about the town's official status.[35] In addition to contrasts between public buildings, attention might also be drawn to the difference between the orthogonal street grid of the eastern hill and the more organic grid of the western.[36]

When, and in particular why, public buildings were abandoned or demolished requires study. The deliberate demolition of London's public buildings in the 3rd and 4th c. can be observed in many other buildings as well.[37] Masonry from such buildings has been found re-used in many late defensive structures, such as the town wall in the early 3rd c., the riverside wall in the mid- to late 3rd c., and bastions added to the wall in the mid 4th c.[38] It is as if there was money for large 'public' (or monumental) buildings, or for large defensive structures, but not for both. This pattern is repeated throughout the province.[39] It has been

---

35 J. Morris, *Londinium, London in the Roman empire* (London 1982) 104; J. J. Wilkes, "The status of Londinium," in *Interpreting London* 27-31; Millett (supra n.13). Southwark should probably be considered as a third separate area. Note the possible Flavian *mansio* (fig. 2, site 27) (C. Cowan, "A possible mansio in Roman Southwark: excavations at 15-23, Southwark Street, 1980-1986," *TransLonMiddxArchSoc* 4 [1992] 3-191), and a possible official residence at Winchester Palace in Southwark (supra n.29). It is increasingly clear that Southwark, with its own public buildings, needs to brought into the debate as more than just a suburb. The construction of the later town wall has, by excluding it, greatly hindered consideration of Southwark's rightful status, just as, by incuding them, it has obscured the differences between the western and eastern hills. Cowan points out that recent findings "challenge the traditional interpretation of Southwark as a low status suburb of Londinium and suggest that at least parts of the civil and military administration were sited on the south bank of the river" (Cowan, ibid. 183).

36 Millett (supra n.13) 433-34.

37 For example, the Cheapside baths (fig. 2, site 5) were abandoned in the 3rd c. (Perring [supra n.2] 77), and most of the buildings in the so-called Governor's Palace complex (cf. supra n.5) were demolished in the late 3rd or early 4th c. (Perring, ibid. 113).

38 Milne (supra n.5) 77, 83-85.

39 Wacher and Frere interpreted the program of wall construction as purely functional, possibly the result of imperial responses to uncertain times. Millett, on the other hand, sees the pouring of huge local resources into

suggested that the abandonment and careful demolition of the Huggin Hill bath-house was the product of a mid 2nd-c. contraction of the population. However, if this had been the only reason, surely other large buildings would have been rendered equally superfluous? The demolition of the only known classical temple in *Londinium* to create the palace of an imperial pretender possibly owes more to politics and symbolism than to the economics of building maintenance or population decline. On the other hand, the razing of the forum to create an empty space is unexplained, unless it was simply to liberate large quantities of building material for defences. But if this was the case, what kind of 'city' was being defended?[40] The time is right for a major re-appraisal of all such 'public' buildings and the implications of their location and scale, builders and occupants, uses and disuses.

---

defensive structures as a classic example of competitive civic munificence (Millett [supra n.25] 139). Evidence now suggests that Southwark continued to flourish outside the 'defended' area in the late 3rd and early 4th c., which suggests that the construction of walls did not have the psychological effect of 'cutting off' Southwark that one might have expected. Construction of public buildings in *Londinium* did not entirely cease after the mid 2nd c.: an octagonal Romano-Celtic temple, itself possibly of the late 2nd c. (Old Bailey site excavated in 1988; see fig. 3, site 17) was replaced after *c.*270 by a possible *mansio* which lasted until the mid 4th c. (Milne [supra n.5] 75, 82).

40   Note that Wacher advised caution when interpreting empty spaces: "it is extremely dangerous to consider vacant building sites as evidence from which to conclude that they represent decline, contraction or even decay of the whole town" (J. Wacher, *The towns of Roman Britain* [London 1995] 96).

The Jubilee Line excavations: recent work on Roman Southwark

Mike Hutchinson

The Jubilee Line Underground Railway Extension excavation was undertaken by MoLAS in advance of the construction of a new ticket hall for the Northern Line beneath Borough High Street. The investigations commenced in May 1995 and were carried out in stages in five separate areas. Work took place directly beneath a temporary artificial road deck over the High Street and continued until November 1995. The site measured 60 m N-S by 15 m E-W, with eastern extensions into St. Thomas Street and the site of 31-39 Borough High Street (fig. 2, site 15).

Early settlement

A large section of the early Roman settlement in Southwark, lying east of the main road leading to London bridge, was uncovered. The excavation revealed two minor lanes or alleys running east from the line of the main Roman road.[1] Ruts made by wheeled vehicles, probably carts, were visible in the surface of one alley or lane. The Roman road and possibly the street pattern as a whole may have been constructed by c.50. Between the alleys narrow timber-framed and clay buildings were constructed, evidently fronting on the main road. Some of these strip buildings had wooden floors and most had a series of hearths, mainly domestic cooking hearths, although several examples were associated with iron waste and may have been industrial. The buildings in this part of the first settlement probably functioned as a series of workshops, shops, and houses.[2]

By 70 these structures had been destroyed by a major fire and the burnt débris spread across the site. The date and scale of destruction suggests that when the rebel forces led by Boudicca destroyed the

---

1   A. H. Graham and P. Hinton, "The Roman roads in Southwark," in *Excavations in Southwark 1973-76, and Lambeth 1973-79* (London & Middx Arch. Soc. and Surrey Arch. Soc. Joint Publication 3, 1988)19-24.

2   Similar early Roman strip buildings have been found on many sites in London: see D. Perring "The buildings," in D. Perring, S. Roskams and P. Allen, *Early development of Roman London west of the Walbrook* (CBA Res. Rep. 70, 1991) 67-107.

newly established settlement of London,[3] they may also have crossed the Thames and made an unrecorded attack on Southwark. The Borough High Street excavations may provide the first evidence for a possible assault south of the river, though we should keep in mind that the light industrial usage of these rows of timber buildings could point to an alternative cause for the fire. Whatever the cause, the site was levelled after the fire and left open, as evidenced by wells and pits dug through the remains. One of these wells contained a miniature amphora that may have been used for wine-tasting or possibly for unguents.

Later settlement

The settlement was rebuilt in the late 1st c./early 2nd c. Further clay and timber buildings and also masonry buildings were constructed next to re-aligned minor roads; their frontages no longer abutted directly onto the main road but stopped some 5-6 m E of it. This created an open gravelled area adjacent to the road which may have functioned as a 'pedestrian precinct' or open market area. Several of the timber buildings featured raised wooden floors of which charred planks and joists survived. One beam slot contained a large quantity of carbonized bread wheat which showed signs of processing, suggesting that the building functioned as a bakery or shop. Associated with another building were several pits and dumps containing large quantities of butchered bone, possibly indicating the presence of a butcher's shop. Additional hearths occurred to the rear of the late 1st- and early 2nd-c. buildings. To the east and at the rear of the buildings were open areas or yards which contained two timber-lined wells and several rubbish pits.

Early in the 2nd c. several masonry buildings replaced the earlier clay and timber buildings. One of them was almost certainly a blacksmith's forge. A complex sequence of hearths was recorded, and the excavation recovered considerable amounts of slag as well as tiny fragments of hammerscale, the small particles of metal produced by hammering hot metal into shape on an anvil. The floors were generally of clay or low-quality mortar, pointing to a low-status or utilitarian function for the buildings.

---

3   Tac., *Ann.* 14.30; the archaeological evidence is discussed by R. Merrifield, *London, city of the Romans* (London 1983) 52-55 and D. Perring, *Roman London* (London 1991) 22-23.

To the west of the buildings, two series of isolated masonry blocks ran N-S. They appeared to be free-standing. A tentative interpretation is that they may have supported the columns of an arcade alongside the road. Certainly there were no associated walls or evidence of internal occupation nor any road surfaces. However, external gravel surfaces suggest that between the frontage of the buildings and the road there was a series of masonry bases. In addition, there was a sequence of linear features running N–S with a large number of associated post-holes. They appeared to be structural and possibly represented road-side fences or palisades, though there were indications of more substantial masonry foundations. A timber palisade perhaps enclosed part of the settlement to the west or east. These features produced a very large number of coins which indicated a 3rd- or 4th-c. date for the latest of them.

Publishing Roman Southwark: new evidence from the archive

Andrew Westman

Southwark saw much redevelopment in the 1980s, and the Museum of London's former Department of Greater London Archaeology (DGLA) sought to conduct excavations where this activity threatened archaeological deposits.[1] There was usually enough money from developers and public sources to finance the fieldwork, but not always enough to analyse the finds, environmental samples, and stratigraphic records, and publish a considered interpretation. The results of excavations in the previous decade had been published adequately,[2] but a backlog of post-excavation work built up on the sites examined in the 1980s. Since 1991 English Heritage has provided the newly-formed Museum of London Archaeology Service (MoLAS) with funds to work through this backlog and prepare publications.

The backlog totals some 70 sites, both large and small, over a wide area south of the Thames. The sites considered here lie in the W part of the island on which most of Roman Southwark was situated. Clearly we cannot publish all these sites at once, but this can be turned to our advantage for the results of analysing the first excavations can inform work on the later ones.

A timber warehouse

The first of our publications appeared in 1996.[3] The excavation was

---

1   See, for example, K. Heard, H. Sheldon and P. Thompson, "Mapping Roman Southwark," *Antiquity* 64 (1990) 608-19.
2   Namely, a report on a single water-front site downstream of London Bridge, and two large collections of reports on a total of 16 other substantial sites: H. Sheldon, "Excavations at Toppings and Sun Wharves, Southwark, 1970-1972," *TransLonMiddxArchSoc* 25 (1974) 1-116; J. Bird, A. H. Graham, H. Sheldon and P. Townend (edd.), *Southwark excavations 1972-1974* (London & Middx Arch. Soc. and Surrey Arch. Soc. Joint Publication 1, 1978); and P. Hinton (ed.), *Excavations in Southwark 1973-76 Lambeth 1973-79* (London & Middx Arch. Soc. and Surrey Arch. Soc. Joint Publication 3, 1988). A third collection of reports on several of the more recent sites had been in preparation when, in 1991, the DGLA was merged into MoLAS, working in the City of London as well as in much of the rest of London.
3   T. Brigham *et al.*, "A Roman timber building on the Southwark waterfront, London" *ArchJ* 152 (1995) 1-72.

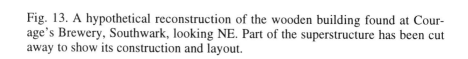

Fig. 13. A hypothetical reconstruction of the wooden building found at Courage's Brewery, Southwark, looking NE. Part of the superstructure has been cut away to show its construction and layout.

one of several on the site of the former Courage's Brewery, west of London Bridge. In 1988 a team from the DGLA uncovered, recorded, and lifted the timbers of an exceptionally well-preserved timber building (fig. 2, site 6). The floor planks were still in place on joists, the ends of which were fitted into the baseplates of the walls. The lower part of one wall, clad with planks, was found where it had collapsed. Originally the building was half sunk in the ground and entered by a ramp from ground level. The roof was probably a simple pitched roof covered with oak shingles (fig. 13).

Careful conservation of the timbers has permitted essential information to be obtained recently. Dendrochronological study has determined, for example, that the baseplates were made from oaks felled in 152 or early in 153. Measurements at different places on the timbers reveal the growth patterns of the trees. The joists all came from coppice stems, indicating the existence of well-managed woodlands near London.

The building was situated on reclaimed land, close to the contemporary riverfront, and would have been damp. The absence of the débris of carpentry implies that the building was pre-fabricated and assembled on site. There were no artefacts to suggest its function, and almost no signs of wear and tear. The best explanation seems to be that it was a warehouse for perishable foodstuffs. It probably constituted a rather modest investment, perhaps by a private trader.

Ironworking

Other excavations at Courage's Brewery provide material for a study of Roman iron-working and copper-working.[4] The evidence was abundant: 70 hearths, masses of slag and spent fuel, and much hammer-scale. Remarkably, iron smithing started early in the life of the Roman settlement, about 70, and continued almost uninterrupted for some 300 years until the end of Roman occupation. This site therefore contains one of the longest sequences of metal-working known in Roman Britain.

Numerous small workshops were built with timber posts or shallow clay and timber walls and perhaps roofed with shingles (like the timber warehouse). These structures sheltered one or two hearths each, on which the raw material was heated. Iron probably arrived in the form of bars and billets, and was then fashioned either hot or cold. We

4   F. Hammer, *Industry in north-west Roman Southwark: excavations at Courage's Brewery, 1964-90* (in preparation).

have almost no evidence of the objects produced. Some material seems to have been collected for recycling but no other artefacts were found, whether partly formed or as waste.

Based on experimental smithing using Roman techniques, it has been possible to estimate how much space the workers would have needed and how many people could have been at work at any one time. Charcoal was apparently the main fuel used, although coal was used as a supplement. The author's experiments lead us to believe that smiths would have occasionally added coal to their hearths to give a more intense and more stable heat.

The charcoal, like the raw iron, probably came from the Weald of Kent and Sussex, by the roads that converged on Southwark and the bridge over the Thames, or by boat down the local tributaries of the Thames. A large iron industry in the E half of the Weald is believed to have supplied the Roman army in Britain and on the Lower Rhine. Perhaps the W half of the Weald, lying closer to London, supplied iron to Southwark. There is no evidence that Southwark's workshops were supplying the army. London would have been an important market for local products, but the intensity and frequency of construction and pitting seem to indicate that iron-working was carried on regardless of fluctuations in the town's economy.[5] This impression is based on a small sample of information but, if accurate, may suggest that Southwark's smiths were manufacturing for a market beyond London itself.

Military connections with Southwark

Some connections can be made between Southwark and the army, however. Specialists at MoLAS have plotted the distribution in SE Britain of tiles stamped CLBR, *Classis Britannica*, a branch of the army responsible for collecting river-tolls and suppressing piracy. These tiles are characterized by a distinctive fabric which has been found in Southwark with or without the stamp, both in original contexts and re-used. Presumably this stamp was proprietory. One may guess that the re-appearance of military building materials in a non-military context may have been the result of misappropriation. This sort of tile is more rarely found on the N bank of the river in London, unlike other re-used tile with a different official stamp, PPBRLON, denoting the office in London of the procurator of the province of Brit-

---

5   See, for example, P. Marsden and B. West, "Population change in Roman London," *Britannia* 23 (1992) 133-40.

ain.[6] The procurator was the chief civil official in the province, responsible mainly for finance, while the governor was the military commander and chief magistrate, with responsibilities which would have kept him on the move. The procurator would have settled in one place more quickly, and by 70 London was probably the procurator's base. The governor at least had an entourage of *beneficiarii consularis* (legionaries seconded to him as note-takers, record-keepers, tax collectors, and executioners). Some evidence connects either military or civil official institutions and personnel with another site in Southwark, at Winchester Palace, between the metal-working area and London Bridge.

Material found at Winchester Palace in layers of fill dated to 60-70 contained large quantities of débris from a substantial masonry building, presumably a bath-house, with water-pipes, vaulted ceilings, heated rooms, and painted wall-plaster of high quality (fig. 2, site 33). The plaster was relatively unabraded and cannot have travelled far; thus, it must have come from a nearby building. At such an early date, the quality of the material marks the building as exceptional, probably constructed under official auspices. It may have been destroyed in the Boudiccan revolt.

In the 2nd c., a bath-house was built on the Winchester Palace site itself, with under-floor heating and, again, wall-paintings of high quality, matching those in the richest Italian villas of the day.[7] The débris from the demolition of the bath-house also contained a high proportion of pig bones, indicating a high-status diet. A marble inscription, dated on stylistic grounds to the 3rd c., was found broken in the débris.[8] The fragments were found close together and presumably cannot have travelled far. The inscription lists men by cohort in the arrangement and numbers appropriate for *beneficiarii consularis*, according to its original interpretation; certainly the inscription implies some kind of military connection with the site (see Yule and Rankov, below).

The post-excavation work[9] has revealed an urban landscape somewhat different from that on the N bank of the river. In NW Southwark buildings were pulled down and re-developed wholesale, as if large

---

6   I. Betts, "Procuratorial tile stamps from London," *Britannia* 26 (1995) 207-29.
7   S. Mackenna and R. Ling, "Wall paintings from Winchester Palace site, Southwark," *Britannia* 22 (1991) 159-71.
8   M. Hassall and R. Tomlin, "Inscriptions from Roman Britain 1984," *Britannia* 16 (1985) 317-22.
9   B. Yule, *Roman buildings on the Southwark waterfront: excavations at Winchester Palace, 1982-90*, I (in preparation).

areas of land belonged to one owner. When fragments of buildings seen in different trenches are plotted together, extensive yet coherent complexes of buildings emerge. The principal range of buildings, to which the bath-house at Winchester Palace was simply an adjunct, may have lain directly to the north, fronting the river. This frontage may have exceeded 100 m in length.

Large-scale analysis and reconstruction

The first publications arising from the sites in Southwark were geographically limited in scope. Today, however, we possess a critical mass of analysable data, and the potential of the remaining unpublished sites suggests possibilities for discussion on a broader and more thematic basis. Indeed, many issues important to environmental research and the finds can only be satisfactorily approached at this level. There is every reason therefore to include more up-to-date information in the next publications, addressing themes such as the origin, development, contraction, and abandonment of the settlement on the south bank of the river, as well as its port, economy, religion, and burial practices.

MoLAS has also assessed data from more recent excavations, notably those carried out for the extension of the Jubilee Line of the London Underground. We could not analyse all these data without an electronic data-base, nor could we use this data-base to advantage unless it would include spatial information in a geographical information system (GIS), derived ultimately from the plans made during excavation. The many questions we wish to ask of a GIS could be answered easily, and the process would discern significant patterns, follow up clues, refine successive questions, and judge the answers.

Publications do not have to be just books and articles. Several reconstructed bird's-eye views of Roman London were prepared[10] for a recent refurbishment of the Museum of London's Roman Gallery. The results illustrate vividly what publishing the backlog means. Topographical reconstruction depends on the accuracy of individual details recorded during excavation, such as the position and alignment of roads and buildings. Such reconstruction also includes conjecture, which is always subject to later revision in the light of new evidence or re-interpretation of old data. Conjecture, as in projecting the line of roads or the extent of buildings, has to be systematic, rational, and controlled, yet brought to life with imagination. Such post-excavation work is as crucial as the original excavations. It yields new information which allows us to fill in, piece by piece, the picture of Roman Southwark — or rather, that part of Roman London which lay on the south bank of the Thames.

---

10   By Dave Bentley, MoLAS Drawing office.

Legionary soldiers in 3rd-c. Southwark

Brian Yule and Boris Rankov

During the archaeological excavations on the site of Winchester Palace (fig. 2, site 33) on the riverfront at Southwark (1983-84),[1] 27 fragments of a fine marble inscription were recovered. The inscription was published in 1985 by M. Hassall; it indicates the presence of legionary soldiers in early 3rd-c. Southwark,[2] yet archaeological evidence for a fortress at Southwark is lacking. In order to understand what a detachment of legionaries might have been doing on the south bank of the Thames at that date, we will present the archaeological context followed by an alternative interpretation of the inscription.

The archaeological context

The earliest land use on the site dates to c.A.D. 60. It comprised infrastructure works — revetment of the waterfront, drainage of land, and road construction. A significant portion of the make-up dumps laid down in advance of building construction was ceramic building material from a demolished building, including voussoir tile from a vaulted ceiling and flue tile from a heated room. Their size and the lack of abrasions on the tiles suggests they had derived from a pre-Boudiccan masonry building which had stood close by. The pre-Flavian and earliest Flavian buildings constructed in the area of our excavation were standard clay-and-timber buildings with mortar floors and rather plain decoration.

The area saw a major redevelopment in c.80. Land was reclaimed and the riverfront advanced to the north. The most interesting ingredient in the dumps relating to the reclamation was fine painted wall-plaster, an indicator of a high-status building nearby. South of

---

1   The excavations on the site of the mediaeval palace of the Bishops of Winchester were carried out by the Museum of London in advance of redevelopment of the Victorian warehouses adjacent to St Mary Overy Dock. Post-excavation analysis of the stratigraphy, finds, and environmental data has now been completed, and the report is forthcoming (B. Yule, *Roman buildings on the Southwark waterfront: excavations at Winchester Palace, London, 1983-1990, Part 1*).

2   M. W. C. Hassall and R. O. Tomlin, "Roman Britain in 1984. II. Inscriptions," *Britannia* 16 (1985) 317-22, no.1.

Fig. 14. The hypocausts and *caldarium* of Building 14, looking south. The fragments of marble inscription were recovered from the stoking pit backfilled with rubble seen to the left of the flue (at point "i"). The masonry walls on the left side and at the rear of the view are part of the mediaeval palace which overlay the bath-house; the 3 large concrete blocks are modern stanchion bases (MoLAS).

the riverfront the road-system was re-organized and a large masonry building with raised floor and a circular (?) building, possibly with a tower, were erected. Neither of these buildings can be paralleled. The current interpretation favours warehouses or granaries, but we cannot rule out the possibility of non-utilitarian heated rooms.

The area was again redeveloped in *c*.120. All earlier structures were demolished and the area was levelled up. Fig. 15 shows the proposed ground-plan of the complex in the 3rd c. There is only very limited evidence for the main riverfront building (Building 12). Building 13 was a well-appointed, heated suite of rooms. A large slab of painted wall-plaster from the lunette of a partition wall in the SE room reveal-

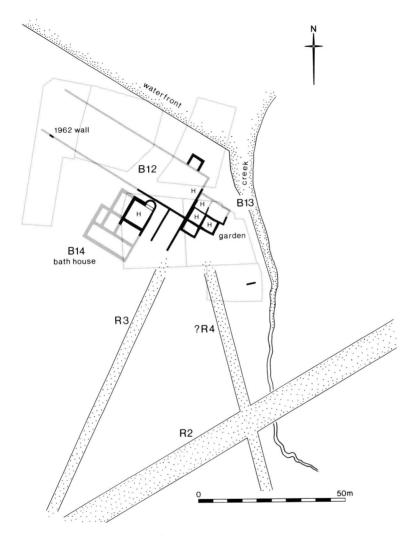

Fig. 15. Conjectural plan of the 3rd-c. building complex (B 12-14) and associated roads (R 1-2) excavated at Winchester Palace, Southwark. The excavated walls are shown in black, conjectural walls in grey. The presence of hypocausts is indicated by "H".

ed a mid 2nd-c. painting of the highest quality.[3] Building 14 was a well-preserved *caldarium* measuring 6.8 m square internally, with attached heated plunge pool[4] (figs. 14-15). It postdated an external dump dating to *c.*150-250. Internal decoration included marble veneers from the Mediterranean and painted wall-plaster with striped decoration resembling the second-phase painting in Building 13; it is generally typical of 3rd-c. wall-painting in Italy. There is evidence for a reconstruction of the hypocaust of the *caldarium,* not closely dated.

The marble inscription was recovered from demolition rubble found in the stoking pit of the hypocaust of the *caldarium,* dating to some time after 287; the latest date is provided by 3 coins of Carausius. The bath-house and part of the heated suite were demolished in the late 3rd-early 4th c., but the complex continued to be used and coin finds suggest that Roman occupation continued into the third quarter of the 4th c.

The site sequence points to continuing high-status occupation within or adjacent to the area that fell within our excavations. The implied heated masonry building dating before 60 is remarkably early for such a building anywhere in London. Early Flavian painted wall-plaster was amongst the finest from 1st-c. Britain,[5] while the mid 2nd-c. painting has its best parallels on the Continent.[6]

Suggestions of a military or official presence also run through the sequence. The high proportion of Claudian irregular coins is in line with the evidence from the rest of the Southwark settlement and has parallels in pre-Flavian military supply dépôts like Fishbourne and Sea Mills.[7] Voussoir tile, present at Winchester Palace in the pre-Flavian make-up dumps and incorporated in the 2nd-3rd c. building complex, is another indicator of military occupation.[8] Official stamped tile — PPBRILON of the Procurator of the Province of Britain,[9] and

---

3   S. A. Mackenna and R. Ling, "Wall paintings from the Winchester Palace site, Southwark," *Britannia* 22 (1991) 159-71.

4   The hypothesized layout follows the plan of the bath house at Vindolanda on Hadrian's Wall (I. Nielsen, *Thermae et Balnea* [Aarhus 1990] fig. 140.

5   R. Goffin, "Roman wall plaster" in Yule (supra n.1).

6   Mackenna and Ling (supra n.3).

7   M. J. Hammerson, "The coins" in J. Bird, A. H. Graham, H. Sheldon and P. Townend (edd.), *Southwark excavations 1972-74* (London & Middx Arch. Soc. and Surrey Arch. Soc. Joint Publ. 1, London 1978) 587-600.

8   N. Crowley, "Building materials," in Yule (supra n.1).

9   I. M. Betts, "Procuratorial tile stamps from London," *Britannia* 26 (1995) 207-29.

CLBR of the *Classis Britannica*[10] — occurs on the site in small quantities, indicating that it was probably not arriving as fresh consignments. However, the London-wide distribution in particular of the *Classis Britannica* tile may indicate that it went predominantly to sites that had military connections. The marble inscription, with its explicit military association (see below), may well have derived from the bath-house, Building 14, which is clearly larger than a residential suite and second in size only to the Huggin Hill Baths.[11]

The character of the occupation appears to have been of an official or 'public' nature (see Bateman above). Unlike many civilian sites below the modern City of London,[12] there was no adherence to local property boundaries. Each of the three redevelopments of the area of Winchester Palace from the mid 1st c. to the early 2nd c. involved a radically different layout, suggesting that a single authority controlled land-use over an extensive area. Evidence for continuity of settlement through the late 2nd-early 3rd c. runs in marked contrast to civilian sites both in the modern City of London and in North Southwark, where a 'decline' is apparent,[13] but it is consistent with the supposed presence of public buildings on both the north and south banks of the river.[14]

The absence of a legionary fortress at London implies that legionary soldiers would have been brought to the provincial capital for duties associated with the provincial administration, that is, under the auspices of the *legatus Augusti* or governor, who was commander in

---

10   N. Crowley and I. M. Betts, "Three *Classis Britannica* stamps from London," *Britannia* 23 (1992) 218-22; Crowley (supra n.8).

11   P. Rowsome, "85 Queen Victoria Street (Dominant House). Excavation round-up 1989, Part 1: City of London," *London Archaeologist* 6.6 (1990) 165-66.

12   At sites like Newgate Street (D. Perring and S. Roskams with P. Allen, *Early development of Roman London west of the Walbrook* [CBA Res.Rep. 70, 1991] 3-26), successive plans show that buildings followed very closely the ground-plans of earlier structures.

13   H. L. Sheldon, "A decline in the London settlement AD 150-250?," *London Archaeologist* 2.11 (1975) 279-84; S. Roskams, "Conclusions," in Perring and Roskams (supra n.12) 120.

14   D. Perring, *Roman London* (London 1991) 81; T. Brigham, "A reassessment of the second basilica in London, AD 100-400. Excavations at Leadenhall Court 1984-86," *Britannia* 21 (1990) 53-97; C. Cowan, "A possible mansio in Roman Southwark: excavations at 15-23 Southwark Street, 1980-86," *TransLonMiddxArchSoc* 43 (1992) 3-191.

chief of the provincial army and assisted by a staff (*officium*) of seconded legionaries.[15]

The marble inscription

Initial interpretation of the inscription from Winchester Palace suggested three possible contexts for the presence in London of the listed soldiers — "due to some special occasion, or ... they were on garrison duty, perhaps at a military post guarding the nearby bridgehead, or ... they were men seconded from one of the legions in the province to serve on the governor's staff."[16] In a footnote,[17] Hassall made the further observation that "much the largest group of seconded legionaries in the *officium* of the legate were *beneficiarii consularis*, probably 60 in all ... and it is just conceivable that this is a list of members of a guild confined to men of this rank, such as is apparently attested at York, the capital of Britannia Inferior in the early third century."[18]

More recently, the latter interpretation has taken prominence,[19] in part because of doubts concerning the previously accepted attribution of the governor's palace to building remains found under Cannon Street Station.[20] However, the interpretation of the inscription as listing members of a *collegium* of *beneficiarii consularis* cannot stand. Although men seconded to the governor's headquarters undoubtedly remained on the books of both their legion and their cohort within the legion,[21] nowhere do *beneficiarii* or any other members of the governor's staff list themselves by cohort in the fashion of this inscription. *Officiales* were selected individually from all the legions of a province, and those of the rank of *beneficiarius* and above were senior

---

15   M. Hassall, "London as a provincial capital," in *Interpreting London* 19-26.

16   Hassall and Tomlin (supra n.2) 321-22.

17   Ibid. 322 n.7.

18   R. P. Wright, "Roman Britain in 1969. II. Inscriptions," *Britannia* 1 (1970) 307 no.12.

19   B. Yule, "Excavations at Winchester Palace, Southwark," *London Archaeologist* 6.2 (1989) 31-39; Hassall (supra n.15) 22-23.

20   P. Marsden, "The excavation of a Roman palace site in London, 1961-1972," *TransLonMiddxArchSoc* 26 (1975) 1-102 and ibid. 29 (1978) 99-103; Perring (supra n.14) 30-33; G. Milne, "A palace disproved: reassessing the provincial governor's presence in 1st-century London," in *Interpreting London* 49-55.

21   This is demonstrated by a discharge list of *legio VII Claudia* from Viminacium in Moesia Superior and dated to 195, which includes *beneficiarii consularis* amongst members of the first cohort: *CIL* III 14507 a 12; 36; 38.

principales, who were normally promoted either within the *officium* itself or to the centurionate. Most served in the *officium* for several years and at the end of their military careers. Few returned to service with their legions.[22] For these men, their attachment to a particular cohort of the legion was largely irrelevant.

Listing by cohort is, however, well attested for members of an ordinary legionary attachment, as Hassall recognised. The clearest parallel which he cites is a century-strong vexillation of *legio IX Claudia* from Montana in Lower Moesia (now Mihailovgrad, Bulgaria), consisting of men from the first five cohorts of the legion.[23] The nature of the list from Southwark as an ordinary legionary vexillation is placed beyond reasonable doubt by the contents of Fragment (h) (see inset in fig. 16), the significance of which has not previously been recognised. This reads as follows:

...]VS II[...
...]S IX P[...
...]X P PO[...
...]VS II PR[...

The letters are 20-25 mm high, and on the basis of this and the thickness of the marble Hassall ascribes it to the same slab (Slab 2) as the only fragment (a) recovered of the heading. The latter reads as follows:

---

22 D. J. Breeze, "The organisation of the career structure of the *immunes* and *principales* of the Roman army," *BonnJb* 174 (1974) 245-92, esp. 263-78; N. B. Rankov, *The beneficiarii consularis of the western provinces of the Roman empire* (diss., Oxford Univ. 1986) 8-96; J. Ott, "Überlegungen zur Stellung der Beneficiarier in der Rangordnung des römischen Heeres," in *Der römische Weihebezirk von Osterburken* II. *Kolloquium 1990 und paläobotanische osteologische Untersuchungen* (Stuttgart 1994) 233-49, esp. 242-43; id., *Die Beneficiarier* (Historia Einzelschriften 92, Stuttgart 1995) 30-32, 39-59; N. B. Rankov, "The governor's men: the *officium consularis* in provincial admin-istration," in I. Haynes and A. K. Goldsworthy (edd.), *The Roman army as a community* (JRA Suppl. forthcoming).

23 *CIL* III 7449, cited by Hassall and Tomlin (supra n.2) 321 with n.6; cf. R. Saxer, *Untersuchungen zu den Vexillationen des römischen Kaiserheeres von Augustus bis Diokletian. Epigraphische Studien* I (Köln–Graz 1967) 89-90, no. 265; N. B. Rankov, "A contribution to the military and administrative history of Montana," in A. G. Poulter (ed.), *Ancient Bulgaria: papers presented to the International Symposium on the Ancient History and Archaeology of Bulgaria, Univ. of Nottingham 1981* (1983) 40-73, esp. 52-54.

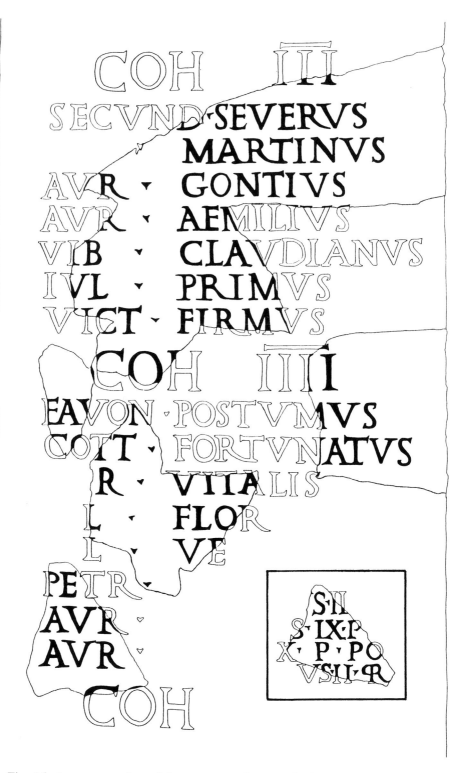

COH III
SECVND·SEVERVS
MARTINVS
AVR · GONTIVS
AVR · AEMILIVS
VIB · CLAVDIANVS
IVL · PRIMVS
VICT · FIRMVS
COH IIII
FAVON · POSTVMVS
COTT · FORTVNATVS
R · VITALIS
L · FLOR
L · VE
PETR ·
AVR ·
AVR ·
COH

S·II
S·IX·P
X · P · PO
VS·II·R

Fig. 16. A reconstruction of the most complete panel of the inscription from Winchester Palace, listing soldiers by numbered cohort. The insert shows a fragment attributed to another panel, recording centurions listed by their relative ranking in cohorts II to X (scale 1 : 4).

...]M et S[...
...]runt[...
...]I̦ Philippu[s

The first two lines are in letters 60 mm high and are evidently part of the main heading of the inscription, while the third line is in letters 22 mm high and is clearly part of a name or list of names which must be separate from the main lists, Fragments (b)-(g), arranged by cohort, which Hassall attributes to Slab 1 (see fig. 16). On these, the letters used for the names of the men in the main lists are 25-28 mm (Fragments (c)-(g)) and up to 30 mm (Fragment (b)) high respectively, and those used for the subheadings indicating cohorts are estimated by Hassall at *c*.42 mm high.

The letter sizes on Fragment (h) allow the possibility of identifying it as part of the list of names which appears to be inserted immediately below the main heading. That this fragment, too, is part of a list of names is made certain by the fact that it bears the abbreviation for centurions arranged by position and cohort. The text is to be expanded as follows:

...]us (secundus) [p(ilus) pr(ior) ...
...]s (nonus) p(ilus) [pr(ior) or po(sterior) ...
...] (nonus) or (decimus) p(ilus) po(sterior) [...
...]us (secundus) pr(inceps) [pr(ior) or po(sterior) ...

The indication of a centurion's title by use of a numeral together with his position within the relevant cohort is well attested epigraphically,[24] but the appearance of several men listed in this way and in this order undoubtedly sheds new light on the long-running debate concerning the relative ranking of legionary centurions in cohorts II to X. In the present context it also makes it certain that we are dealing with a vexillation from one of the legions of Britannia Superior (if we accept the presence of several Aurelii in the lists on Slab 1 as indicating a 3rd-c. date[25]) — that is, a vexillation of *legio II*

---

24   See M. P. Speidel, "The centurions' titles," *EpigStud* 13 (1983) 43-61 (= id., *Roman army papers* vol. 2 [Stuttgart 1992] 21-30); id., "The names of legionary centurions," *Arctos* 24 (1990) 135-37 (= *Roman army papers* vol. 2, 40-42); cf. id., "Rangzeichen fur Zenturionen und die Grosse Weiheinschrift aus dem Mainzen Legionslager," *JbRGZM* 33 (1986) 321-29 = *Roman army papers* vol. 2, 43-55; J. C. Mann, "Roman legionary centurial symbols," *ZPE* 115 (1997) 295-98.

25   Hassall and Tomlin (supra n.2) 322.

Augusta from Caerleon or of *legio XX Valeria Victrix* from Chester. Both the number of centurions and the way in which they are designated is quite inappropriate and unparalleled for a list of *officiales*, but is entirely suited to a vexillation drawn from several cohorts. The number of centurions also means that the vexillation is likely to have been of a substantial size, despite the fact that Fragment (c) appears to list only 7 men from *cohors III*. As Hassall points out, the Montana vexillation has 5 men from *cohors II*, 8 men from each of *cohors I and cohors II*, 9 men from *cohors IV*, but 37 men from *cohors V*.[26]

Conclusions

The reason for the presence of such a vexillation in London must remain unclear in the absence of further sections of the heading. We might, however, add one possibility to those adduced by Hassall, namely that they were a building detail. The use of troops, and especially legionaries, for building work is well known, although this was much more narrowly restricted to military and governmental construction than has been generally recognised.[27] That the inscription records construction of a government building (e.g., bath house and ? — *balnea]m et S*[?) in Southwark by a large detachment of legionaries brought in by the governor is as plausible an interpretation as any.

Significantly for the interpretation of the riverfront of the south bank, the archaeological context shows that legionaries in the 3rd c. need not have been alien to the area. The Roman sequence provides evidence of high-status buildings with military associations from the earliest date. These buildings are assumed to be 'official', that is, connected with the provincial administration. Whether this makes Winchester Palace a contender for the site of *the* governor's palace is

---

26   Ibid. 321.
27   R. MacMullen, "Roman imperial building in the provinces," *HSCP* 64 (1959) 207-33, but note that almost all the building work tabulated on p.218 was done for use by the military or was carried out, often in provincial capitals, at the behest of the governor; id., *Soldier and civilian in the later Roman empire* (Cambridge, MA 1963) 23-48. On building work carried out by vexillations, see Saxer (supra n.23) 126, and note in particular his no. 294 = *CIL* 6627 = *ILS* 2483, an inscription of the early principate from Coptos in Egypt which records a vexillation of 6 men taken from each cohort of two legions (probably *III Cyrenaica* and *XXII Deiotariana*), together with several hundred auxiliaries, making 1401 men in all, engaged in the construction of roads (probably), as well as road-side cisterns and a fort.

uncertain, as the physical organisation of the administration in the western empire is not well understood. It is unclear whether governor and staff would have been housed in a single large complex, as apparently at Cologne and Aquincum,[28] or billetted at a number of addresses on the north and south banks of the Thames.

28   See I. Richmond's survey of Roman provincial palaces in I. A. Richmond (ed. P. Salway), *Roman architecture and art* (1969) 260-79, esp. 266-69.

Cathedrals, granaries, and urban vitality in late Roman London

David Sankey

Late Roman London is under-represented in the stratigraphic record. This paper reviews some new findings in a large late 4th-c. building in the SE part of the Roman town, and suggests that urban life may have been more vibrant at that period than is often supposed.

The degree to which the late 3rd- and 4th-c. town of London was occupied and inhabited has been obscured by the later re-working of the archaeological deposits to form a buried soil.[1] Perring, for example, suggested a figure of 100 houses in the early 3rd c. and even fewer by the end of the 4th.[2] I believe that this is too small a figure and that the 4th-c. town was both larger and more vigorous than his figures suggest. As most Roman buildings in London were constructed of clay and timber, the increase in the number of masonry buildings in later Roman times may be the result of differential preservation, since stones cannot easily be broken down. Thus, it is the large monumental structures to which we must turn for an indication of urban conditions and activity.

Aisled building at Colchester House

Near the SE corner of the town, excavations between September 1992 and January 1993 revealed a large aisled building (fig. 3, site 7), built after 350, as shown by pottery of Portchester D type found in significant quantities beneath it. The building was located on a small hill which had been levelled to 10.0 m asl, and it sat astride the end of one of the main E-W roads which crossed the Roman town. It had an external wall foundation 2 m thick; its trench had been dug down to natural gravels and thousands of wooden piles or stakes had been inserted, a difficult (and probably unnecessary) engineering feat because of the compressive strength of the gravel. Over the gravels was spread a layer of charcoal and clay, followed by one of chalk and knapped flint, carefully packed around the top of the piles. On top was poured a layer of concrete to support a stone structure (subsequently robbed).

---

1 B. Watson (below, p. 102) has suggested one possible mechanism, but I believe that the same effect could be produced by the excavation of trenches to get rid of nightsoil (ash and human waste) at any point in history when the ground was open.

2 D. Perring, *Roman London* (London 1991) 127.

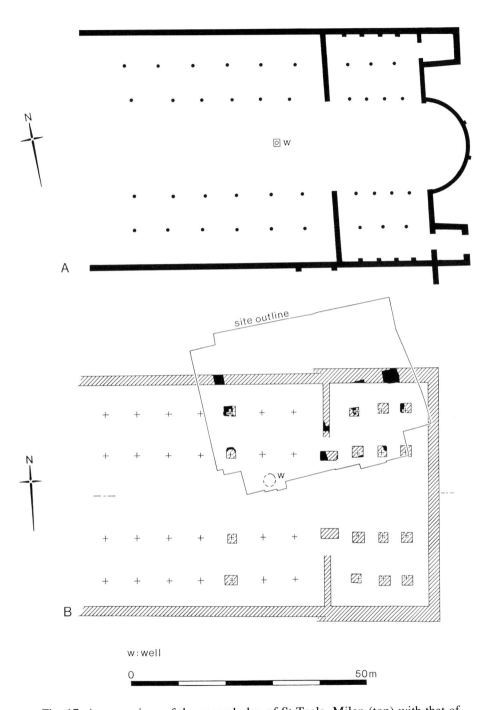

N

A

N

B

site outline

w

w : well

0   50m

Fig. 17. A comparison of the ground plan of St Tecla, Milan (top) with that of the excavated remains of the foundations found at Colchester House, London (bottom), both drawn to the same scale. Note particularly the relationship between the wells (w) and the internal walls, and the variable spacing of the columns at St Tecla, which are set further apart to the west of the internal wall than to the east of it. Such an arrangement would fit the London evidence better than one with uniform spacing on either side of the internal wall.

An internal wall of similar construction, though slightly narrower, ran at 90° to the external wall (fig. 17). On either side of the internal wall was a series of pad foundations (2 x 2.5 m), again of the same construction. One, however, lay beyond the end of the internal wall out of line with the other pad foundations. The floor of the building consisted of a layer of rubble, followed by poured rough concrete and a further layer of finer concrete screed over which re-used tiles and thin sandstone slabs provided a fine finish. The building may have possessed marble decoration and window glass, but only a few fragments were recovered and they came from secondary contexts. A well located at the edge of the site was filled with the only material from the demolished building not subsequently removed; it also included a dispersed coin hoard (not yet conserved or dated).

This small part of what was clearly a much larger building parallels closely in plan and scale a part of the late 4th-c. cathedral of St. Tecla at Milan (fig. 17) when Milan was an imperial capital. Notwithstanding the limitations of the evidence from London, certain details underline the comparison. The relationship of the well to the internal wall is the same in both cases. If the pad foundations west of the internal wall at London followed the spacing of the pillars which lie west of the internal wall at St. Tecla, they too would have produced a regular series. Both the pillars east of the wall at St. Tecla and the pads east of the division in the London building are more closely spaced than those to the west, a spacing which would not have produced a regular series if reproduced west of the wall. Even a notable departure from the St. Tecla plan, the extra pad at the end of the internal wall, fits with the reconstruction of the London building as a church, since it could have served as the foundation of an arch which often marked the division between the sanctuary and the rest of the interior.

This similarity of plans is very strong: it is rare to encounter buildings of apparently the same dimensions when comparing ground plans. However, before claiming that the cathedral of Roman London[3] has been discovered, we should consider alternative functions. The London

---

3   The Acts of the Council of Arles in 314 list among the attendees a bishop of London as well as other bishops, a presbyter, and a deacon from Britain. The relevant text is reproduced in J. Ireland (ed.), *Roman Britain: a sourcebook* (2nd ed., London 1996) 204. C. Thomas has suggested that by the end of the 4th c. the church in Britain had a fully developed hierarchy with metropolitan bishops, and that the major towns would have required a full complement of both congregational and proprietary churches: see C. Thomas, *Christianity in Roman Britain to A.D. 500* (London 1981) 191-200.

building was not a civil basilica, since by this period civil basilicas were constructed to a smaller scale, as at Trier where there was no aisle at all. In any event, encounters between state functionaries and the general population at this date tended to be mediated by the church, which preferred to use generously-sized places of worship. An alternative function is that of a series of state *horrea* (granaries) of the kind used to store the *annona* (tax in kind).[4] In the late Roman period, they were large, aisled masonry buildings, sometimes with an internal wall, although the pillars are normally equidistant on either side of the division, and wells are located in a central courtyard, not within the building itself.

Either reconstruction, as a *horreum* or a church, has similar implications for the status of Roman London in the late 4th c. Such structures are found only in important strategic and metropolitan centres. *Horrea* of this type have been found in Milan, Trier, and Aquileia. Those responsible for commissioning the London building evidently had ambitions for the town as a strategic centre, even if those ambitions were subsequently disappointed.

Other construction programmes

The large building found in the SE part of the town was not the only major engineering project completed in the late 4th c. Around the eastern half of the town a series of external towers or bastions was added to the Wall, constructed over an existing ditch which had been backfilled and replaced by a new, broader ditch dug further out. The bastions have been dated by a coin of Constans (341-346) found in the backfilled ditch at Dukes Place; pottery and bronze coins of 364-375 were found within deposits that had accumulated up against the external face of bastion 6.[5] Excavation has demonstrated that certain of the corresponding bastions on the western side of the town are not earlier than mediaeval in date, though since here the original ditch was backfilled and a new one dug further out, as at Ludgate,[6] one may question why it

---

4   They are unlike earlier *horrea*. The ascription for the building in Trier derives from a toponym.

5   J. Maloney, "The discovery of bastion 4A in the City of London and its implications," *TransLonMiddxArchSoc* 31 (1980) 68-76; J. Maloney, "Recent work on London's defences," in J. Maloney and B. Hobley (edd.), *Roman urban defences in the west* (CBA Res. Rep. 51, 1983) 108.

6   P. Rowsome, *Excavations at 1-6 Old Bailey (1985)* (unpublished archive report, Museum of London).

was done if no bastions were built at the same time. It is certain that the entire circuit of the town's defences was reinforced; it was not merely a reduced *castellum* or point of refuge. This was in marked contrast to the majority of Gallic towns in which walls constructed at this date normally enclosed only a fifth or even as little as a tenth of their original extent.[7] The erection of a new stretch of the river wall at what is now the Tower of London also dates to the end of the 4th c. It was a substantial construction over 3.2 m wide with a timber, rubble, and poured concrete core faced with re-used masonry (fig. 3, site 24).[8]

Burials are another type of evidence, and they are not subject to the destructive forces which afflict clay and timber buildings. Recent work on the cemeteries of East London shows no evidence of any reduction in the rate of burial in the 3rd and 4th c.[9] Though information from other cemetery excavations has not been similarly analysed, there is no mortuary evidence to support a significant decline in population.

This evidence is relevant to one final consideration: how vigorous was urban life at the end of the 4th c.? The first issue is clearly population size. If the building found in the SE part of the town was a church basilica, and if the size of such structures bore a similar relationship to town size as had the size of earlier civil basilicas, one would conclude that London had declined in population by about a third. Such a decline would be comparable with the toll of the Black Death in the mid 14th c. and would not have amounted to a catastrophic decline, though it would have caused serious social disruption. The second question is how strategic a centre was London. Then and for centuries afterwards it controlled transport and communications both along and across the Thames valley. Even if it was no longer the thriving trading centre that it had been in the earlier Roman period, it was the capital of a diocese and provided the springboard for imperial ambitions. Its name was changed to Augusta, possibly reflecting an enhanced status. The whole urban area was regarded as worth defending, at very considerable cost and effort. In the 4th c., in some respects (e.g., its defended area) London was a more vigorous centre than many cities of the western empire, whatever its subsequent fate.

---

7   S. Johnson, "Late Roman urban defences in Europe," in *Roman urban defences in the west* (supra n.5) 69-76.

8   G. Parnell, "The Roman and medieval defences and later development of the inmost ward, Tower of London: excavations 1955-77," *TransLonMiddx ArchSoc* 36 (1985) 21.

9   Bruno Barber, pers. comm.

Roman London:
recent finds and research

Angela Wardle

Elsewhere in this volume aspects of current work on the development of Roman London are discussed largely from an architectural, economic, or spatial viewpoint. Here attention will be focused on finds from some of the sites. Roman finds have generally been published by site;[1] there is no comparable companion to the successful series of publications on mediaeval finds.[2] Recent large-scale excavations, which have produced rich assemblages, and current work on the unpublished backlog have created opportunities to reconsider how to publish finds and to evaluate the importance of artefacts in understanding the material culture and development of London. In this paper examples from several contrasting sites are employed to illustrate the direction and scope of current research.

At No. 1 Poultry (fig. 2, site 20), a complex multi-period site lying on the W side of the middle Walbrook valley in the heart of Roman *Londinium*, waterlogged deposits near the stream bed have preserved finds well. Both copper alloy and iron artefacts have survived in superb condition, as illustrated by a rare plate brooch in the form of a ship (fig. 18). In common with many of the artefacts from deposits near the Walbrook, the brooch is complete and undamaged.[3] Parallels for this type can be found in other NW provinces. Other objects of particular intrinsic interest include a copper alloy lamp complete with hanger, a Bacchic figurine carrying bunches of grapes, a finely worked eagle's wing also from a figurine, and a mount in the shape of a leaping

---

1   For example, D. M. Jones and M. Rhodes, *Excavations at Billingsgate Buildings 'Triangle', Lower Thames Street, 1974* (London & Middx Arch. Soc. Special Paper 4, 1980); L. Miller, J. Schofield and M. Rhodes, *The Roman quay at St Magnus House, London* (London & Middx Arch. Soc. Special Paper 8, 1986); G. Milne and A. Wardle, "Early Roman development at Leadenhall Court, London, and related research," *TransLonMiddxArchSoc* 44 (1993) 23-170. For a more general work, see G. Milne, *The port of Roman London* (London 1985).

2   For mediaeval finds, see the DUA/MoLAS series, *Medieval finds from excavations in London*, vols. I-V.

3   E. Ettlinger, *Die römischen Fibeln in der Schweiz* (Bern 1973); J. Garbsch, *Mann und Rofl und Wagen: Transport und Verkehr im antiken Bayern* (Munich 1986).

Fig. 18. A copper-alloy plate brooch in the form of a ship, found at No. 1 Poultry (length 28.5 mm).

female panther, which is likely to be either from a piece of furniture or the fitting of a vehicle (fig. 19); panthers and other subjects drawn from the Bacchic *thiasos* were commonly used for such a purpose.[4] Iron implements, also well preserved in the anaerobic conditions, include tools, knives, razors, and over 50 iron *styli*. Several *styli* are decorated with mouldings or non-ferrous inlay and at least two are stamped. One of these appears to be identical to an elaborate stamped example from the Walbrook now in the Roach Smith Collection, although it has not yet been possible to read the stamp.[5]

The finds from No. 1 Poultry are currently being examined to assess their contribution to the site and their wider significance, following procedures advocated by English Heritage.[6] Apart from many items of intrinsic interest, the groups from the Walbrook will be of considerable value in furthering debate about the nature and purpose of the finds from the Walbrook stream and its surroundings. The latest contribution

---

4   Four protomes from Athens in the form of panthers are shown in E. von Mercklin, "Wagenschmuck aus der römischen Kaiserzeit,," *JdI* 48 (1933) 84-176. I am grateful to C. Johns for this reference.

5   W. H. Manning, *Catalogue of the Romano-British iron tools, fittings and weapons in the British Museum* (London 1985) 66 n.7.

6   English Heritage, *Management of archaeological projects* (1991).

Fig. 19. A group of artefacts from No. 1 Poultry. Two copper alloy brooches, a mount in the form of a panther, and an iron knife illustrate the superb condition of the metalwork.

to this debate, made by the late R. Merrifield,[7] challenged the view of the deposits as simple rubbish disposal and argued for a strong element of ritual.[8]

As with the earlier collections from the Walbrook, the groups contain many implements in pristine condition; the *styli*, greater in number than from other London sites, are also notable. Analysis of the stratigraphic position of these artefacts is still in its preliminary stages but this is a rare opportunity to study a well-documented and well-stratified assemblage. The boat-shaped plate brooch described above (fig. 18) typifies the interpretative problems likely to be encountered at a later stage of the analysis. The form of the brooch highlights the potential for investigation of the range of designs employed for plate brooches, a subject raised recently by C. Johns,[9] who pointed out that since the size of the brooches precluded practical use as fasteners, and though likely to have been worn as decorative objects, such forms of decoration might possess a significance not readily apparent to the modern viewer. The subject of this brooch, the strong Celtic element in the design, and its location in a dump on the banks of the Walbrook raise many interpretative possibilities: perhaps it was a casual loss, perhaps a votive offering? Interpretation of the Walbrook dumps, however, cannot rely solely on analysis and comparison of the non-ceramic finds; integrated study all components of the assemblage, including both ceramic and environmental evidence, is essential.

Organic finds, sometimes a casualty of previous investigations of the Walbrook, have been well preserved and well conserved at No. 1 Poultry. A notable collection of writing tablets, several with traces of script, complements the *styli*, while other wooden artefacts include boxes, bowls, a shovel, and the base of a wooden chest. Barrels, some stamped, are proving useful in the study of ancient wood-working techniques and the re-use of timber.[10] An unusual discovery was the top of a shale table. Among the many preserved leather artefacts are some

---

7   In the Hugh Chapman Memorial Lecture: R. Merrifield, "Roman metalwork from the Walbrook — rubbish, ritual or redundancy?," *TransLonMiddx ArchSoc* (forthcoming).

8   T. Wilmott, *Excavations in the middle Walbrook valley* (London & Middx Arch Soc Special Paper 13, 1991); C. Maloney with D. de Moulins, *The upper Walbrook valley in the Roman period* (CBA Res. Rep. 69, 1990).

9   C. Johns, "Mounted men and sitting ducks: the iconography of Romano-British plate brooches," in B. Raftery (ed.), *Sites and sights of the Iron Age* (Oxford 1995) 103-9.

10   Undertaken by Damian Goodburn.

pieces that may be from furnishings or upholstery. The remaining leatherwork consists chiefly of shoes and displays a useful range of styles current in the 1st and 2nd c., but there are also fragments of seams which may derive from briefcase-like containers.[11]

Sites near the water-front have also produced notable collections of leatherwork. A group of 1st-c. shoes from Suffolk House (fig. 2, site 28), including one with an eagle stamped on the sole, complements the group from No. 1 Poultry and earlier collections from sites on the water-front.[12] Although there was military presence in London, these appear to be essentially civilian items, and comparison with collections outside London, particularly from sites in N Britain such as Vindolanda, would be of considerable interest. Among the large number of finds from Regis House (also on the water-front, fig. 2, site 24), is an important group of leather artefacts with military associations, including large fragments of tents. Warehouses on the same site have also provided new evidence for commercial activity, including glass-working. One of the most intriguing discoveries was a group of three lead ingots buried beneath the floor, each bearing the official stamp of Vespasian.[13]

Numerous military items from the new sites include a remarkable fragment of *lorica squamata* now on display in the Museum of London, buckles and hinged straps from body armour, studs, mounts, several cavalry harness pendants and, again from No. 1 Poultry, several spear-heads and butts. Metalwork from inland sites is generally less well preserved but at Bishopsgate (fig. 2, site 3) a cheek-piece and crest box and plume holder from an infantry helmet were recognised. It is hoped that the new finds will be included in the corpus of military items now being prepared for publication by the Museum of London.[14]

---

11   Carol van Driel Murray (pers. comm.), who has also commented on the group from Regis House.

12   Previous publications of leather from London include the important early group from Billingsgate Buildings (M. Rhodes in Jones and Rhodes [supra n.1] 99-128, and later material from New Fresh Wharf (P. MacConnoran in Miller *et al.* [supra n.1] 218-26).

13   M. Hassall and R. Tomlin, "Roman Britain in 1995," *Britannia* 27 (1996) 446-48. Further work by Dr. M. Dearne has confirmed their source as Charterhouse-on-Mendip (see also T. Brigham *et al.*, "Current archaeological work at Regis House in the City of London," *London Archaeologist* 8 [1996] 31-44).

14   M. Bishop *et al.*, *Corpus of military objects from Roman London* (Museum of London monograph, forthcoming).

Fig. 20. A copper alloy *balsamarium* from 7-11 Bishopsgate, front and back views (height 60 mm).

Artefacts with Bacchic associations were mentioned above in discussion of the groups from No. 1 Poultry, and such items occur with some regularity on London sites. The finest of the most recent discoveries is a *balsamarium* (incense or oil container), also from Bishopsgate, found in débris from a 3rd-c. fire (fig. 20a-b). The flask, in the shape of the bust of a youth with exotic, perhaps Ethiopian, features, rising from a calyx, has affinities with others found in Britain and Europe.[15] With

---

15 J. Webster, "A bronze incense container in the form of Bacchus from Carlisle," *TransCumbWestAntArchSoc* 73 (1973) 90-93; V. Hutchinson, *Bacchus in Roman Britain* (BAR, BS 151, Oxford 1986) 22, 228-29. For further examples of *balsamaria* with Nubian features, see G. Faider-Feytmans, *Les bronzes romains de Belgique* (Mainz 1979) 126-27, pls. 87-90.

the increasing numbers of Bacchic objects in London, a review of evidence for the cult is due.

Studies of finds in London are not confined to the town itself, nor to current excavations. Hitherto all major publication in Southwark has been arranged by site, with separate short catalogues of finds for each site.[16] English Heritage has recently funded work on a cluster of sites at Courage's Brewery (fig. 2, site 6), where there is important evidence of industrial activity.[17] Current work on the assessment of sites in Southwark excavated between 1972 and 1991 has entailed the examination of several large and varied assemblages of finds and many smaller groups. This programme has created a unique opportunity to consider together a substantial area of this important settlement, and a number of thematic proposals aimed at a greater understanding of the development, economy, and changing character of the area are being considered. Study of the artefacts is an integral part of this exercise. Furthermore, finds from the earlier excavations have been usefully supplemented by those from the work associated with the Jubilee Line Extension, notably at Borough High Street (fig. 2, site 15), where there is a long sequence of occupation with evidence of commercial and industrial activity.[18] Excavation continues in Southwark, and the recent discovery of burials flanking Watling Street adds to our developing knowledge of finds from the cemeteries of Roman London, another area of recent research.[19] Given the wealth of material from sites of differing character, the potential for research on finds is great.

---

16   J. Bird et al. (edd.), Southwark excavations 1972-74 (London & Middx Arch. Soc. and Surrey Arch. Soc. Joint Publication 1, 1978); C. Cowan, "A possible mansio in Roman Southwark: excavations at 15-23 Southwark Street, 1980-86," TransLonMiddxArchSoc 43 (1992) 3-119; B. Yule, Roman buildings on the Southwark waterfront: excavations at Winchester Palace, 1983-90, I (in preparation).

17   C. Cowan, The development of north-west Roman Southwark: excavations at Courage's Brewery, 1964-90 (in preparation); F. Hammer, Industry in north-west Roman Southwark: excavations at Courage's Brewery 1984-88 (in preparation).

18   P. Hinton (ed.), Excavations in Southwark 1973-76, Lambeth 1973-79 (London & Middx Arch. Soc. and Surrey Arch. Soc. Joint Publication 3, 1988).

19   J. Hall, "The cemeteries of Roman London: a review," Interpreting London (1996) 57-84. The eastern cemetery is the subject of a recent project: B. Barber and D. Bowsher, The eastern cemetery of Roman London: excavations 1983-90 (in preparation).

Pottery publications and research in Roman London

Louise J. Rayner and Fiona Seeley

Through the work of MoLAS and its predecessors, the Departments of Urban Archaeology (DUA) and of Greater London Archaeology (DGLA), there has been continuity in the approach to the study of Roman pottery. Sites in the modern City of London and in the Borough of Southwark directly opposite the City produce very large assemblages of pottery, often in securely stratified deposits. The identification of horizons, such as the Boudiccan fire that can be dated to 60-61 by literary sources, has provided a chronological framework for Roman pottery, while research has also been aided by the excavation of well-preserved timbers from the Roman riverside. The timbers have yielded very accurate dendrochronological dates which have dated not only the structures but also the large dumps of pottery used to consolidate the revetments. Recent publications and research have built upon the DUA's emphasis on fabric identification[1] and methods of quantification,[2] and the DGLA's creation of a typology of forms[3] and

---

1   B. Davies and P. Tyers, *Neronian pottery from London: a study of the pre-Boudiccan pottery from the General Post Office site, Early Roman pottery from the City of London* I (Unpub. Archive Report, Museum of London 1983); B. Davies and P. Tyers, *Highgate B and allied fabrics from London: their chronology and typology, Early Roman pottery from the City of London* II (Unpublished Archive Report, Museum of London 1983); B. Davies, *Highgate C fabrics from London: their chronology and typology, Early Roman pottery from the City of London* III (Unpublished Archive Report, Museum of London 1983); P. Tyers, *Verulamium region type white ware fabrics from London, Early Roman pottery from the City of London* IV (Unpublished Archive Report, Museum of London 1983); A. Chadburn and P. Tyers, *Early Roman pottery from Fenchurch Street, Early Roman pottery from the City of London* V (Unpublished Archive Report, Museum of London 1984); B. Davies, *Imported and Romano-British fine wares, Early Roman pottery from the City of London* VI (Unpublished Archive Report, Museum of London 1984).

2   C. Orton, "Introduction to the pottery reports," and "Roman pottery," in T. Blurton, "Excavations at Angel Court Walbrook 1974," *TransLonMiddx ArchSoc* 28 (1977) 28-53.

3   G. Marsh and P. Tyers, "The Roman pottery from Southwark," in J. Bird *et al.* (edd.), *Southwark Excavations 1972-74* (London & Middx Arch. Soc. and Surrey Arch. Soc. Joint Publication 1, 1978) 533-82.

publication of securely dated groups.[4] All excavated pottery is 'spot-dated' by context. This involves the examination of all sherds with a x20 binocular microscope in order to identify the fabric. Codes for fabric, form, and decoration are recorded, with sherd count, comments, and an early and late date for each context. The information is entered into a relational data-base and these data form the basis for analysis and research. The aim of this article is to summarize recent and forthcoming publications on Roman pottery in London, and current and future research.

Recent publications

A corpus of early Roman pottery from the City of London[5] presents typological and chronological groups of Roman pottery dating from 50 to 160. The material included was recovered from excavations in the City, supplemented by complete vessels from the reserve collection of the Museum of London. The first part of the corpus sets out typological groups under four broad headings: Amphorae, Oxidized wares, Reduced wares, and Fine wares. For every fabric there are detailed sections on petrology, dating, technology, source and typology. The range of forms for each fabric is fully illustrated. The second part of the corpus presents a chronological overview of early Roman pottery in London. Six dated ceramic phases, from pre-Boudiccan to Early Antonine, are discussed and illustrated with an overview of ceramic trends, maps of source areas, and graphs showing the relative proportions of wares. The groups presented cover the main Romano-British industries supplying London in the early period, most importantly the kiln sites of Verulamium (Hertfordshire), Highgate Wood (10 km north of the City), and Alice Holt (Surrey), as well as imported fine wares and amphorae. The corpus is of value to a wide audience because an extensive range of pottery has been found in London. The colour plates include photographs of sherd breaks to aid comparison and identification of wares.

The recent report on Roman pottery from Leadenhall (fig. 2, site 17) develops research aims and themes initiated in earlier reports,[6]

---

4   M. Hammerson, "Roman pottery," in P. Hinton and H. Swain, *Excavations in Southwark 1973-6, Lambeth 1973-9* (London & Middx Arch. Soc. and Surrey Arch. Soc. Joint Publication 3, 1988) 193-294.

5   By B. Davies, B. Richardson, and R. Tomber (CBA Res. Rep. 98, 1994).

6   G. Milne and A. Wardle, "Early Roman development at Leadenhall Court, London and related research," *TransLonMiddxArchSoc* 44 (1996) 23-169.

including further refinement of the dating of late 1st-c. assemblages described in the early Roman corpus.[7] Detailed analysis of groups from well-stratified deposits suggests that the changing quantities of reduced fabrics are key indicators for dating assemblages to the early, middle and late phases of the period 70/75-100. In a multidisciplinary study, the authors attempt to examine questions concerning the function, socio-economic status, and level of Romanisation of the site. Several approaches are used, including analysis of the distribution of fine wares in relation to specific buildings or areas to indicate high, middle and low status, and comparison of proportions of vessel types to examine levels of Romanisation. The records of the spot-dating (noting presence or absence) are used to look at the extent of the early settlement and the socio-economic patterns of the later 1st c. A study of the distribution of different forms and wares shows a high proportion of amphorae, not only around the port, as might be expected, but also in the area of the forum, indicating that the forum may have been a site where amphora contents were redistributed.

An article which examines Roman ceramics from 140 to 400 and beyond[8] complements the early Roman *Corpus*. Five quantified groups are presented from three sites in London, detailing the types and quantities of wares, discussing forms and dating evidence, and providing catalogues and illustrations. Two broader sections examine Late Roman pottery in London in the context of regional pottery supply and in the context of Late Roman London. The study identifies three main trends: a continuity in supply from the Early Antonine period until *c.*200; the influx of late Alice Holt grey wares from *c.*270; and the increase of Oxfordshire products and calcite-gritted ware in the 4th c. The study of Late Roman ceramics in London is still developing, particularly when contrasted with our understanding of the early period, and the article concludes with recommendations for future study. The most important of these is the overall refinement of dating for the later 2nd and 3rd c., which requires further groups to be examined.

Forthcoming publications

A forthcoming publication focuses on a large assemblage from Ironmonger Lane (fig. 2, site 14) dated to the mid- to late 2nd c., a per-

---

7   *Corpus* (supra n.5).
8   R. Symonds and R. Tomber, "Late Roman London: an assessment of the ceramic evidence from the City of London," *TransLonMiddxArchSoc* 42 (1994) 59-99.

iod when some of the major ceramic industries supplying coarse wares to London were declining.[9] A catalogue of vessels dating to the Late Roman period will be published in a volume on the Roman cemeteries of East London.[10] Much of our analysis of pottery is based on quantification and the methodology is constantly reviewed in response to funding constraints, especially because a site in London can produce several tons of Roman pottery. As part of the forthcoming publications on NW Southwark (fig. 2, site 6),[11] a comparative study has been made of the following types of quantification: presence or absence of types using spot-dating records, estimated vessel equivalents, and weight.

Projects

In addition to publications, MoLAS is involved in a number of British and European projects.[12] The creation of a National Roman Fabric Reference Collection has been undertaken, with funding from English Heritage. The collection, housed at the British Museum, includes over 600 sherds whose fabrics are being described and thin-sectioned. A paper outlining the project has been published and the resulting publication is in final preparation.[13] A second project funded by English Heritage is the compilation of a bibliography of *mortarium* studies.

Recently MoLAS has also become involved in three European projects. Two projects are part of the European Commission's 'Raphaël' programme. The first is titled *CAESAR: Validation project for archaeological ceramics at European Atlantic ports*, while the second project is a data-base for Samian wares from Lezoux. The third project will work towards the creation of an 'International Reference Collection for Ceramics of the Roman Period in Western Europe' if funding is made available by the European Community.

---

9   R. Symonds, "A large group of 2nd-c. pottery from Ironmonger Lane, in the City of London: IRL 95, context 58," *Journal of Roman Pottery Studies* (forthcoming).

10   R. Symonds in B. Barber and D. Bowsher, *Roman London: the eastern cemetery* (forthcoming).

11   P. Rauxloh and R. Symonds in C. Cowan, *The development of north-west Roman Southwark: excavations at Courage's Brewery, 1964-1990* (forthcoming).

12   We are grateful to our colleagues Roberta Tomber and Robin Symonds for information regarding their projects.

13   R. Tomber and J. Dore, "A national Roman fabric reference collection," *Britannia* 27 (1996) 368-82.

Future publications and research

Throughout 1996 and 1997, work has been progressing on the spot-dating and assessment of ceramic assemblages from both current developer-funded excavations and 'backlog' excavations funded by English Heritage. The assessment of these sites has led to a proposed programme of publications[14] which will improve knowledge of chronological periods that remain poorly understood, and address important thematic questions with a view to presenting a more coherent picture of Roman London and Southwark. Thematic research includes the early Roman occupation of London and evidence for pre-Roman activity through the identification of pre- and early post-conquest ceramics, a study of the distribution of imports (especially amphorae) from the waterfronts, to examine the patterns of trade between London and the empire, an analysis of the redistribution of amphorae within the settlement,[15] and a multi-disciplinary approach to the study of ritual and religious activity in London and Southwark, encompassing human cremation and burial, and ritual deposits and rites.

The functional analysis of vessels is a methodological approach recently introduced in London. Analysis using a Geographical Information System to produce intra-site and inter-site spatial patterning will contribute to discussions on the status and function of areas across London and its hinterland. The main chronological study required is the continuation of work on Late Roman pottery, primarily by extending the Southwark typology[16] to include late forms and by publishing securely dated assemblages.

The formulation of our current research aims has been made possible by previous work and analysis that have been briefly summarised above. Detailed chronological and typological studies have provided a base for thematic analysis. The current emphasis is on a multi-disciplinary approach, in which Roman pottery can contribute to the overall picture. Ongoing research will continue to refine the existing base of knowledge for Roman pottery in London and will no doubt emphasise further areas requiring study.

---

14   L. Rayner and F. Seeley, in *Roman Southwark* (Unpublished Archive Report, Museum of London 1997).

15   A continuation of research detailed in the report on Leadenhall Court (supra n.6).

16   Marsh and Tyers (supra n.3).

New evidence for the ritual use of animals in Roman London

Jane Sidell and Kevin Rielly

Data collected from rescue excavations in the 1980s and 1990s have been combined to form a single research project studying the layout and use of the eastern Roman cemetery[1] (fig. 3). A number of deposits contained faunal remains which were considered to be of ritual derivation.[2] This paper highlights some of the problems in the study of palaeo-environmental samples from the cemetery and briefly describes the results obtained.

Burials of the 1st c. are scarce, being found in areas such as Newgate and Bishopsgate.[3] It was not until the late 1st or early 2nd c. that the eastern cemetery came into use.[4] This cemetery represents the largest group of human remains studied from *Londinium* and is thought to have continued in use until the early 5th c. During excavation it became clear that a proportion of the animal bones came from within the graves. Other animal remains were present within isolated features that did not appear to be the result of a 'practical' activity, such as the disposal of domestic or industrial waste that has been clearly identified across the cemetery. Animal remains were also found in cremations. The ritual use of animals in cremations represents a practice continued from the Iron Age, whereas the presence of animal bones in inhumations is rare in Iron Age burials.[5] Grant has identified a significant change in the use of animals in religious rites in the Roman period, as seen at the shrine at Uley, Gloucestershire.[6]

1   B. Barber and D. Bowsher, *The eastern Roman cemetery, London* (MoLAS Monograph Series, forthcoming).

2   K. Rielly, "The animal bones," in Barber and Bowsher (supra n.1); E. J. Sidell, *Assessment of the animal remains from the East London Roman Cemetery* (Unpublished Archive Report, Museum of London 1993).

3   B. Jones and D. Mattingly, *An atlas of Roman Britain* (London 1990) 301.

4   B. Barber, D. Bowsher and K. Whittaker, "Excavations of a Roman cemetery of Londinium," *Britannia* 21 (1990) 1-12.

5   A. Grant, "Animals in Roman Britain," in M. Todd (ed.), *Research on Roman Britain 1960 to 1989* (Britannia Monograph 11, 1989).

6   B. Levitan in A. Woodward and P. Leach (edd.), *The Uley shrines: excavations of a ritual complex on West Hill, Uley, Gloucestershire, 1977-9* (1983).

Inhumation ritual

Only 3% (19) of the graves found in the London cemetery contained animal grave goods. Most contained chicken and pig; in three cases goose bones were present. The dominance of chicken and pig bones corresponds to the evidence gathered in Lauwerier's study of food offerings within 15 Roman cemeteries in Europe.[7] A number of inhumations in Lauwerier's study also contained the bones of geese. In Britain, however, the grave goods recovered from inhumations at other Roman cemeteries often include pig and chicken bones, but more frequently they contain cattle and sheep/goats.

The offerings in London appears to deviate slightly from the pattern established by Lauwerier's study, in which almost all offerings encountered in graves were presented as 'meals'. It is difficult to establish whether such meals were placed with the body as offerings, or whether they were traces of meals eaten during funerary feasting, later added to the burial. The presence of articulated bones accompanied by a plate or vessel seems to be the best indication of the former. A number of the offerings in the cemetery appear to be *in situ*, Several other examples can be cited. Bones of domestic fowl from Hooper Street[8] were recovered in ceramic vessels which probably served for storage. This may be associated with a belief that sustenance was needed after death. At 65-73 Mansell Street, a grave contained a piglet split into halves, one of which was accompanied by a whole goose, while most of a chicken was placed with the other half. The size of this offering suggests that explanations other than that animal remains in burials represent offerings of meals should be sought. Although it has been stated of this cemetery that "the act of burial need not necessarily reflect religious belief,"[9] it seems likely that a religious significance can be attached to this group. Cultic significance can be attributed to certain animals such as chickens, which have been associated with Mercury[10] who guided the spirits of the departed to the underworld. A tentative suggestion therefore is that the Mansell Street assemblage could have derived from a religious sacrifice and served as an offering of food to the individual.

7　A. Lauwerier, "Bird remains in Roman graves," *Archaeofauna* 2 (1993) 75-82.

8　A. R. Pipe, *The animal bones from Hooper Street* (Unpublished Report, Greater London Environmental Archaeology Service 1992).

9　Barber *et al.* (supra n.4).

10　M. Henig in Todd (supra n.5).

Cremation ritual

Both burnt and unburnt animal bones were more commonly found with cremations than inhumations, occurring in c.50% of cremations. This relatively high figure contrasts with Philpott's study of British cemeteries, which indicated that a small number of cremations contained animal remains.[11] It seems unlikely that this difference is associated with any change between 'paganism' and Christianity. No direct evidence of Christianity was recovered from the excavations, and inhumations were found from the earliest phases of the cemetery, although in lower numbers than cremations. The difference is also unlikely to be a factor of preservation, which is variable spatially across the cemetery, and may be associated with later truncation.

Chicken and pig are again the dominant burnt species in the London cemetery, a further difference from Philpott's study which indicated that cattle and sheep/goat remains were most common in British cremations, although pigs and birds have been recovered. A large proportion of the chickens from the London cemetery include the majority of the carcass, while the pig bones may point towards use of legs only. One of the more interesting aspects of the unburnt animal bones is the unusually high proportion of fish bones.[12] Fish are not recorded in Philpott's study of cremation practices in Britain, nor at other European sites. This implies that the fish were offerings from feasting within the London cemetery, and were added to the human remains after cremation. Despite an extensive programme of sieving, individual fish species in each cremation were generally composed of no more than 5 fragments, the vast majority of which were vetebrae.

These patterns suggest certain Roman ideas about burial ideology. First, general food offerings were required during the actual cremation of the body and then they were included with the parts of the body which were buried. Almost certainly some animal bones will have been left on the pyre, as indicated by the deposits of probable 'pyre débris' found in the cemetery. Second, additional uncremated offerings accompanied the cremated body. Thus formal offerings were thought to be needed for the afterlife, but there was also a 'gesture' made, with the offerings on the pyre viewed as the necessary sustenance. For

---

11   R. Philpott, *Burial practices in Roman Britain: a survey of grave treatment and furnishing* (BAR BS 219, Oxford 1991).

12   M. Grunewald, *Der römische Nordfriedhof in Würms. Fünde von der Mainzer Strasse* (Würms 1990).

inhumations, by contrast, the use of formal articulated offerings and then remnants of a funerary banquet are suggested.

Remains unassociated with human burials

At the outset of the project, it was hoped to identify activities within the cemetery that were associated with funerary rite but distinct from burial rite, such as feasting. At 49-59 Mansell Street, the articulated remains of a horse, a dog and a red deer were placed nose-to-tail in a circle within a pit. This is likely to have been associated with ritual. There is no evidence for their slaughter, but certain species are associated with particular cults, e.g., horses with Celtic deities,[13] dogs with Mithras and a British hunter-god known from a number of representations in London;[14] a stag too is possibly depicted with the latter deity. The three species are an unusual combination, however, and cannot yet be fully explained.

A large pit discovered at St Clare Street contained hundreds of frog and toad bones and the complete skeleton of a heron. Initial suggestions that the group had a ritual significance were countered by the suggestion that the pit had lain open for a period of several months.[15] The presence of a group of complete ceramic vessels and the absence of bone waste have led to a more serious consideration of possible ritual association. Again, however, it is difficult to suggest just what form the rites might have taken, and what purpose they could have served.

A substantial quantity of other bones were found in deposits across the cemetery, the majority considered to be domestic and commercial waste from the town.

Summary

Examination of the faunal assemblage from the East London cemetery has raised a number of points regarding Roman funerary rites. The offerings made with inhumations resemble finds from other

---

13   M. Green, *Religion in Roman Britain* (London 1983).

14   J. Hall and R. Merrifield, *Roman London* (London 1986) 40; R. Merrifield, "The London hunter-god," in M. Henig and A. King (edd.), *Pagan gods and shrines of the Roman empire* (OUCA Monograph 8, 1986) 57-64.

15   Sidell (supra n.2); H. Hibberd, *Amphibian studies in archaeology: an analysis of the small animals from the St. Clare Street pit* (Unpublished MS Thesis, Univ. of London 1991).

European cemeteries[16] in that the dominant species are chicken and pig. This contrasts with evidence from other British sites, and may indicate that *Londinium* was more cosmopolitan than other British towns, and more comparable with European cities. The food species are slightly different from those expected on urban sites, in that pig tends to be less common than other meats, particularly in the later period. Cattle would appear to be the most common species on late Roman urban sites, but some sites, such as Winchester Palace at Southwark,[17] may also contain large quantities of pig, possibly as dietary components of a higher status. However, it must be acknowledged that meat offerings off the bone (e.g., filleted beef) would leave no obvious traces, although such possibilities could be investigated by chemical testing of ceramic vessels. This could result in a revision of the perceived imbalance. Sheep or goat meat is likely to have been kept on the bone, however; thus the low representation of these species cannot be explained by this argument.

Finally, although it has been possible to identify ritual use of animals through conventional faunal analysis, the ideology behind the rites is still far from clear. The death rituals of the inhabitants of Roman London needs further study.

Acknowledgements

The authors would like to thank English Heritage for funding the research project, various private bodies for funding the excavations, and Tony Dyson for his comments on this paper.

---

16   Lauwerier (supra n.8).
17   K. Rielly, "The animal bones from Winchester Palace," in B. Yule, *Roman buildings on the Southwark waterfront: excavations at Winchester Palace, London, 1983-1990, Part 1*) forthcoming.

'Dark earth' and urban decline in late Roman London

Bruce Watson

Late 4th-c. London is poorly understood owing to the incompleteness of the archaeological evidence. Within the walled town the latest Roman deposits have often been removed by subsequent activities, such as the digging of rubbish pits in the mediaeval period or the construction of modern buildings with deep basements. However, later activities have not often disturbed the deeper deposits, creating an archaeological record that is biased in favour of the earlier Roman period.

A recent study of late Roman (3rd-4th c.) pottery from the walled town has identified a number of occupied sites near the bridgehead. The latest pottery on all but one of these sites dates to c.350-400 (fig. 3).[1] On only one site, the Billingsgate bath-house, does the pottery suggest that occupation continued into the 5th c. (fig. 3, site 3).[2] A hoard of 273 coins from this bath-house dates to c.395-402.[3] The distribution of all these sites suggests that by the mid 4th c. large areas of the walled town were either abandoned or sparsely occupied. The apparent abandonment of London's port facility by the mid 3rd c.[4] and the demolition of portions of the basilica during the late 3rd or early 4th c.[5] are indicative of a serious economic decline which would have encouraged depopulation.

---

1   R. P. Symonds and R. S. Tomber with D. Lakin and B. Richardson, "Late Roman London; an assessment of the ceramic evidence from the City of London," *TransLonMiddxArchSoc* 42 (1994) 59-99.

2   P. Marsden, *Roman London* (London 1980) 180-81; Symonds *et al.* ibid. 77. The only other evidence to date of 5th-c. occupation within the area of London are several graves of very late 4th- or early 5th-c. date (B. Barber, D. Bowsher and K. Whittaker, "Recent excavations of a cemetery of Londinium," *Britannia* 21 [1990] 11), and a few finds of 5th-c. pottery (L. Blackmore, "Stratified pottery, fifth to seventeenth century," in G. Milne, *St Bride's Church London, archaeological research 1952-60 and 1992-95* [English Heritage Archaeological Report 11, 1997] 54-57).

3   Symonds *et al.* ibid. 61-62.

4   T. Brigham, "The late Roman waterfront in London," *Britannia* 21 (1990) 159.

5   T. Brigham, "A reassessment of the second basilica in London, A.D. 100-400: excavations at Leadenhall Court 1984-86," *Britannia* 21 (1990) 77.

Notwithstanding the severity of economic decline in London during the late 4th c., investment in its defences continued. A series of bastions was added to the E side of the town wall in c.351-75.[6] In the SE corner of the town, a second phase of a defensive wall along the river was constructed in c.390.[7] These investments may be linked with London's important fiscal rôle. In the *Notitia Dignitatum*, a list of officials produced in c.400-425, the diocese of Britain included the 'director' (*praepositus*) of the treasury in London.[8] During the late 4th c., a large building, possibly a *horreum* or warehouse, which could also have served as a treasury, was constructed inside the town (see Sankey p. 81 above, and fig. 3, site 7).

The 'dark earth'

The latest Roman deposits on many sites in London and Southwark consist of a layer of anthropogenic soil (sometimes over 1.0 m thick) known as 'dark earth'. The main components of this soil are silt and fine sand, and its most common inclusions are pebbles, residual rubble and ceramic building material. Deposits of dark earth also occur in other Romano-British urban centres including Canterbury and York, where in all cases the deposits are interpreted as evidence of decline or abandonment.[9]

It is clear that the accumulation of dark earth began at different times in various areas of the walled town. At Milk Street, accumulation begun during the late 2nd c. (fig. 3, site 14),[10] while at Austin Friars in the E side of the town this process did not begin until either the late 3rd or 4th c.[11] It is also clear that the accumulation of dark earth was not always a single, uninterrupted event. Excavations at

---

6   J. Maloney, "Recent work on London's defences," in J. Maloney and B. Hobley (edd.), *Roman urban defences in the west* (CBA Res. Rep. 51, 1983) 96-117.

7   G. Parnell, "The Roman and medieval defences and later development of the inmost ward, Tower of London: excavations 1955-77," *TransLonMiddx ArchSoc* 36 (1985) 21.

8   S. Ireland, *Roman Britain: a source book* (2nd ed., London 1996) 138.

9   P. Ottaway, *Archaeology in British towns* (London 1992) 71, 112-15.

10 S. Roskams and J. Schofield, "The Milk Street excavations, part two," *London Archaeologist* 3 (1978) 227-34; D. Perring and S. Roskams with P. Allen, *Early development of Roman London west of the Walbrook* (CBA Res. Rep. 70, 1991) 49.

11 B. Watson, "Excavations and observations on the site of the Dutch Church, Austin Friars, in the City of London," *TransLonMiddxArchSoc* 45 (1996) 17.

King Street revealed one building, dating probably to the 3rd c., which
was sealed by dark earth, while the construction of an adjoining building during the 4th c. postdated the first accumulation of dark earth
(fig. 3, sites 1, 13).[12] Numerous excavations in London and Southwark
over the last 30 years have shown that there was no simple progression
from early Roman expansion and economic growth to late Roman abandonment and economic decline. The pattern is much more complex. Redevelopment within late Roman London can perhaps be compared to
modern English market towns, in which new supermarkets and derelict
buildings can be found in close proximity.

The interpretation of the 'dark earth'

The interpretation of the deposits of dark earth within London and
Southwark have been the subject of debate for many years. The dark
earth within the walled town was first systematically examined by
W. F. Grimes, who between 1946 and 1968 directed a series of excavations on bomb sites in advance of redevelopment. He identified these
deposits as late Roman and described them as 'sterile soil' or 'a dark
fairly stiff loam ... quite without stratification'.[13] In Southwark, dark
earth was first identified by Kenyon in 1945-47, during excavations on
bomb sites. She suggested that the dark earth in Southwark was built
up from fluvial silts laid down during the 4th c. by successive floods of
the Thames.[14] Further work in Southwark in 1972-74 led to the
conclusion that the dark earth was the result of the dumping of
domestic and organic rubbish on abandoned urban areas to create market
gardens for fruit and vegetables.[15] Currently, the widely accepted
thesis is that, as late Roman London and Southwark progressively
"became less densely occupied, space was turned over to gardens,
market gardens and orchards".[16]

---

12 P. Rowsome, "36-37 King Street, 1985," in J. D. Shepherd, "The pre-urban
    and Roman topography in the King Street and Cheapside areas of the City of
    London," *TransLonMiddxArchSoc* 38 (1987) 46-50.

13 Wartime bombing and V-rocket attacks on London in 1940-44 created many
    vacant sites: see W. F. Grimes, *The excavation of Roman and mediaeval London*
    (London 1968) 122, 127.

14 K. M. Kenyon, *Excavations in Southwark* (Research Paper of Surrey Arch.
    Soc. 5, 1959) 14.

15 H. Sheldon, "The 1972-74 excavations: their contribution to Southwark's
    history," in *Southwark excavations 1972-74*, I (London & Middx Arch. Soc.
    and Surrey Arch. Soc. Joint Publication 1, 1978) 40.

16 D. Perring, *Roman London* (London 1991) 79-80.

There are three fundamental problems with this explanation for the origin of dark earth. Firstly, it would have involved a great deal of work to dump the dark earth on derelict sites in order to make a horticultural soil. At Rangoon Street, the surviving volume of dark earth found in 1982 has been estimated at *c*.300 tonnes (fig. 3, site 18).[17] Second, London was in any event surrounded by excellent farmland, and the creation of urban market gardens cannot have been a serious attempt at self-sufficiency since the town would still have required large amounts of grain and other commodities. Of course, abandoned areas would have made convenient rubbish tips, and after a few years of dumping they could have provided poor quality grazing. For example, after World War II, empty bomb sites were rapidly colonised by many species of plants, even in a densely built-up urban environment.[18]

Lastly, the hypothesis of market gardens is not supported by micromorphological study of the dark earth in London and Southwark.[19] Micromorphological analysis has identified two distinct horizons within deposits of dark earth. The lower one represents the initial build-up, largely derived from the biological re-working (root and worm action) of the upper part of the Roman strata, mixed with dumped material such as ash and cess. The upper horizon of dark earth is always very uniform as a result of biological re-working, and apparently derives from a mixture of natural soil build-up, dumped material, and the re-working of the underlying deposits.[20]

Where pollen has been extracted from dark earth in London (often it is not preserved), there is very little evidence of farming or gardening; rather, the plants represented are characteristic of grassland or urban

---

17 B. Bowler, "Rangoon Street," *Popular Archaeology* 5.6 (1983) 13-18; R. I. Macphail and M. A. Courty, "Interpretation and significance of urban deposits," *Proceedings of the 3rd Nordic Archaeometry ISKOS 5 Finnish Antiq. Soc.* (Helsinki 1985) 71-83.

18 The London bomb sites were rapidly colonised by up to 126 species of flowering plants, shrubs, and ferns: see R. S. R. Fitter, *London's natural history* (London 1945) 265.

19 This study has been conducted by Dr R. Macphail of the Institute of Archaeology, University of London. Soil micromorphology is the analysis of thin sections of soil through optical microscopy, which allows the identification of the soil's parent materials: see M. A. Courty, P. Goldberg, and R. Macphail, *Soils and micromorphology in archaeology* (Cambridge 1989) 261-68.

20 Courty *et al.* (supra n.17) 77; Courty *et al.* (supra n.19) 263-67.

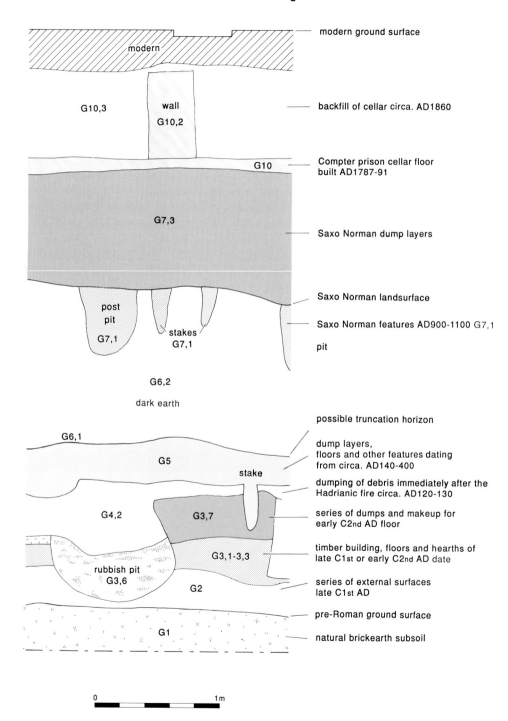

N   S

modern ground surface

modern

G10,3   wall
G10,2   backfill of cellar circa. AD1860

G10   Compter prison cellar floor
built AD1787-91

G7,3   Saxo Norman dump layers

Saxo Norman landsurface

post
pit   Saxo Norman features AD900-1100 G7,1

G7,1   stakes   pit
G7,1

G6,2

dark earth

possible truncation horizon

G6,1

G5   dump layers,
floors and other features dating
from circa. AD140-400

stake   dumping of debris immediately after the
Hadrianic fire circa. AD120-130

G4,2   G3,7   series of dumps and makeup for
early C2nd AD floor

G3,1-3,3   timber building, floors and hearths of
late C1st or early C2nd AD date

rubbish pit
G3,6   G2   series of external surfaces
late C1st AD

pre-Roman ground surface

G1   natural brickearth subsoil

0   1m

Fig. 21. The sequence of archaeological deposits in trench 7, West Yard of King
Edward Buildings. The impressive degree of stratigraphic survival with the dark
earth deposits is due to the fact that basements were never constructed in this area.

wasteland.[21] Analysis of the phyoliths[22] from samples of dark earth in London likewise reveals the presence of wasteland grasses. Samples of dark earth have "produced little clear evidence of cultivation".[23]

Re-analysis of the sequences of early Roman buildings at Newgate Street and Milk Street has led to the suggestion that the late Roman strata have been destroyed by biological re-working and only remain *ex situ* as dark earth. On both sites, many of the late Roman coins were found within either the dark earth or the post-Roman deposits, and post-dated the latest surviving buildings on site.[24]

For many years the greatest hindrance to the study of dark earth in London was the absence of a complete soil profile, owing to post-mediaeval truncation. In 1992, excavations in the yard of King Edward Buildings Royal Mail Sorting Office at Newgate (fig. 3, site 11), unexpectedly revealed a complete 'dark earth' soil profile (fig. 21).[25] The sequence of deposits was: G5, the dumping of domestic rubbish, soil and ash, containing pottery dating to 240-400; followed by G6, a layer of dark earth, 1.2 m thick with clear basal interface which could represent either a possible truncation horizon or simply the downward limit of biological re-working (fig. 21). This soil was derived from the dumping of ash, cess and rubbish, the weathering and biological re-working of the underlying Roman deposits, and natural soil build-up. The deposit was excavated in a series of spits 20 cm thick, and pottery dating from 250-400 was recovered from both the top and bottom levels, suggesting extensive re-working. The only possible structural features within the soil were two post-holes packed with stone. Palynological study confirms that the area was urban wasteland, not garden or woodland. Finally, in G7, the dark earth was sealed by a Saxo-Norman (900-1100) land surface including posts and stakes, which confirmed that by that date the area had been re-occupied.[26]

---

21   R. I. Macphail "Soil and botanical studies of dark earth," in M. Jones and G. Dimbleby (edd.), *The environment of man: the Iron Age to the Anglo-Saxon period* (BAR BS 87, Oxford 1981) 309-31.

22   Phyoliths are tiny biogenic silica rods within the cellular structure of grasses: see Macphail (supra n. 21) 312, 324-25.

23   Courty *et al.* (supra n.19) 268.

24   B. Yule, "The dark earth and late Roman London," *Antiquity* 64 (1990) 620-28.

25   R. I. Macphail and G. M. Cruise, *King Edward Buildings: assessment of soils and pollen (KEB92)* (Unpublished Archive Report, Museum of London 1993).

26   B. Watson, *Report on the Archaeological Evaluation at King Edward Buildings, London EC1 (KEB92)* (Unpublished Archive Report, Museum of Lon-

The soil profile at King Edward Buildings provides a snapshot of late Roman London, at a site which was used intermittently as a rubbish tip during the 3rd and 4th c. by people still living nearby, perhaps adjacent to the main street to the south. Here there appears to have been no re-occupation until c.1000, when people started living above this soil horizon, which during the previous six centuries had been accumulating and was being reworked by biological processes.[27]

---

don 1993).

27   A. Vince, *Saxon London: an archaeological investigation* (London 1990) 19-25.

Epilogue: a view of Roman London from the hinterland

Michael Fulford

The present collection on recent archaeological work and the publication in 1996 of *Interpreting Roman London*[1] are impressive additions to the ever-growing bibliography of Roman London. Given that only a small proportion of the excavations undertaken within and without the Roman town walls and across the river in Southwark over the last 20-30 years has been published — and that only now are the crucially important, post-war excavations by W. F. Grimes of, *inter alia*, the Mithraeum and the Cripplegate fort about to see the light of day as final published reports — we can expect at least a doubling of the modern literature on this unique, provincial Roman town in the next few years.

The present collection and *Interpreting Roman London* offer two contemporary yet contrasting viewpoints on the study of Roman London. This contrast is best illustrated by the fact that four of the papers in the latter (Hassall, Wilkes, Millett and Reece) touch on the evidence for the political and urban status of London. Milne's essay in the latter also touches on wider issues concerning the formation of the city and the establishment of it as the headquarters of the provincial governor. What kind of town was Roman London, was it chartered and if so when, and how we should understand the concept of 'capital'? The debate will be furthered by the new work put forward in the present collection.

Yet it is reasonable to ask what difference the status or rank of the community, whether and when a *municipium* or a *colonia*, would have made to London's physical appearance and vitality. As long as the office of the procurator and the headquarters of the governor remained in London, a certain level of business would have been generated by the attendant bureaucracies of financial and judicial administration, irrespective of the status of the community. Equally, its standing as a major port can hardly have been influenced by its rank. Indeed, there is almost an inverse correlation between its early success as a port, as represented in the archaeological record, and its possible, eventual rise to the rank of *colonia*. It is conceivable that a close examination of the development of Mainz, also a provincial 'capital', but not known to

---

1   J. Bird, M. Hassall and H. Sheldon (edd.), *Interpreting Roman London: a collection of essays in memory of Hugh Chapman* (Oxford 1996)

have had city status before the reign of Diocletian, will reveal parallels with London.[2]

The two books share a further theme in common: that is, for the most part, they present the story of Roman London from a London perspective. Taken as a whole, however, there are serious gaps in both collections. In particular, there is only passing consideration as to how the town might have worked, how it subsisted. There is an important review in *Interpreting London* by Hall of the cemeteries, but there is little reflection in either on the living population of Roman London. Trade and the handling of goods are frequently referred to, but how important were these activities in the changing fortunes of the town? David Bird's paper in the same book on the "London region in Roman times" is the only contribution to take a close look at the relations between the city and its rural hinterland. This *envoi* to a review of recent archaeological work offers the possibility of opening debate and research on two key, but neglected areas.

Let us begin with a comment on physical development (see Bateman above). The exceptional character of the town undoubtedly owes a great deal to the nature of the administrative and judicial offices discharged by it, and to its commercial rôle. So, in one respect, we can point to the growth in provision of public buildings in the town in the aftermath of the Boudiccan revolt and up to the construction of the great forum basilica at the end of the 1st and beginning of the 2nd c., a programme which has no parallel in quantity and quality (as, for example, in the [for Britain] relatively lavish use of imported, coloured marbles) elsewhere in the province. While no neighbouring town would have been without some public building, especially a suite of baths, we should recall how the *civitas* capital of the Atrebates was being provided with a splendid forum basilica in timber at about the same time that work was beginning on its massive sister building in London.[3] Building stone, particularly freestone, was and is at a premium in both places; with London, however, no expense was spared in bringing in material from the Kentish Rag (Lower Greensand) exposed in the Medway Valley in Kent, as well as freestone from further afield. Such provision is followed at the beginning of the 3rd c. by the construction of the town walls which, setting aside the legionary fortresses converted into *coloniae*, were the first in Roman Britain.

---

2   J. C. Mann, "London as a provincial capital," *Britannia* 29 (1998) forthcoming.

3   M. Fulford, "Silchester: the early development of a civitas capital," in (ed.) S. J. Greep, *Roman towns: the Wheeler inheritance* (CBA Res. Rep. 93, 1993) 16-33.

On the other hand, in respect of its rôle as a port, we should remind ourselves that no other coastal or estuarine town or fortress has produced anything approaching the scale of wharf facilities that have been found over the last generation of rescue archaeology in London and Southwark. Brigham documents above the steady investment into London's waterfront such that by the end of the 1st c. timber quays stretched over some 500 m along the N bank of the Thames. With rebuilding and further extensions, by the early 3rd c. the waterfront extended along about 1 km of foreshore. While comparable facilities might have existed elsewhere in the Roman west, we do not yet know of them.

The exceptional civil and commercial rôles of London can be further illustrated in a variety of ways in respect of buildings and material culture, but it is the population which demands further reflection. Let us consider the civil side and the individuals that serviced the offices of the governor and procurator, how their lives were shaped in the town, and how, in turn, they might have shaped the town. The publication of the strength report from Vindolanda which notes the number of soldiers seconded to the governor in London in the 90s[4] reminds us that the length of service in the capital, whether as an ordinary *miles*, or a *beneficiarius consularis*, would have been short, no longer perhaps than the term of service of the governor himself. In respect of its mobility, the population of London was quite different from that of a *civitas* capital. What loyalties would such an appointee to London have had to the community? What kind of investment would he or the provincial governor have made to house himself and, in the case of an officer, perhaps, his family? Was the administrative community different in character to the commercial? Did the latter have closer ties with the town, a sense of belonging which might have sponsored temples and other public buildings, or was the occupation by merchants equally short-lived? Such questions have a peculiar relevance when we consider the situation in the 3rd c. The riverside town wall, which was built in the third quarter of the 3rd c., was constructed of re-used materials, including quantities of limestone ashlar, two altars recording the reconstruction of temples, and a number of blocks representing two decorated monuments.[5] Re-used ashlar was also found in the foundations of a major building, perhaps a palace for the usurper Allectus, constructed

4   A. K. Bowman and J. D. Thomas, *The Vindolanda writing tablets (Tabulae Vindolandenses II)* (London 1994) no. 154.
5   C. Hill, M. Millett and T. Blagg, *The Roman riverside wall and monumental arch in London* (London & Middx Arch. Soc. Special Paper 3, 1980).

after the spring or summer of 294.[6] Not only does the existence of this material point to an area of public building in the SW quarter, but the date of much of the work appears to lie within the 3rd c. Just as earlier the Huggin Hill Baths appear to have been demolished within little more than half a century of their original construction by the mid 2nd c. (Bateman above), so too do the monuments and buildings in the SW of the town. In their case it is not only the context of their original construction, at a period when little public building is being carried on elsewhere in towns within Britain and the Roman West, but also the short period of time in which they stood that deserve comment. Such treatment of public buildings also extends to the great forum basilica which was almost entirely razed to the ground by the end of the 3rd c.[7] In speculating why buildings of this status merited such treatment, we should recall the possibility that the collective memory of London was short, reflecting the brief tenure of officials engaged in provincial business. New governors, or usurper emperors, could choose to demolish their predecessors' work and start all over again. Thus London is not only unique in the way it was provided with major buildings, but also in the way, through successive generations, it treated its heritage. Shortage of materials may have been a driving force as we see the re-use of PP.BRI.LON tiles in later Roman buildings,[8] but the act of construction says much about how the town was regarded. It is possible that the forum basilica was demolished because it represented the early imperial past at a time when the usurpers like Carausius and Allectus were, perhaps, trying to carve out a new identity for themselves. On the one hand, it mattered what was attempted in London in the way of new buildings; on the other, little that was constructed stood the test of time. Nevertheless, it is readily understandable why Constantius Chlorus chose to use the recovery of London on the Arras medallion as his symbol of the recapture of Britannia.

If the above considerations concern the changing physical environment of the town and how a possibly rapidly changing residential population perceived it, we must now turn to the commercial character of London. One of the paradoxes of London's waterfront development is that it did not reach its fullest extent until the early to mid 3rd c., at a

---

6   T. Williams, *Public buildings in the south-west quarter of Roman London* (CBA Res. Rep. 88, 1993).

7   T. Brigham, "A reassessment of the second basilica in London, AD 100-400: excavation at Leadenhall Court, 1984-86," *Britannia* 21 (1990) 53-97; G. Milne, *From Roman basilica to medieval market* (London 1992).

8   I. M. Betts, "Procuratorial tile stamps from London," *Britannia* 26 (1995) 207-30.

time when the archaeological evidence suggests that trade and maritime traffic were much in decline. That evidence for the most part is represented by durable imports and so, perhaps, gives a one-sided picture. Yet the archaeological record of exports of British origin across the Channel at any period is slight.[9] So how can we interpret this material evidence? There is considerable agreement that the flow of imported goods probably included perishable, and thus archaeologically invisible, commodities, and that the relative decline in volume from the 2nd c. onwards represents a slackening of dependence on overseas sources for the supply of the army. Were the imported commodities replaced by goods of British origin and were they handled for overseas delivery, for example to the German frontier, or for routing to the British frontier up the east coast? If London was principally handling imported goods for onward movement by road in the 1st and early 2nd c., how did it fare later when coastal traffic to the north increased, both via the east and the west coasts?[10] That London drew goods from the south and southwest is demonstrated not only by the presence of materials such as Bath Oolite and Purbeck Marble but also by a high tenor of Southeast Dorset Black-burnished pottery.[11] If we accept that these materials can be regarded as tracers of other, perishable commodities or skills (see Henig in *Interpreting London*) coming from the country, then London was more important as a consumer or an outward transmitter (by sea) from the early to mid 2nd c. onwards. The continued and substantial investment into the waterfront suggests strongly to me that London played a major redistributive rôle for both goods coming in from across the Channel and from the countryside of Britannia to serve the northern frontier and, at least from time to time, the German frontier in the 2nd and 3rd c.

An important question, given the scale of the waterfront development, is how important was London as a port in provincial affairs. While other ports can be postulated at other locations around the coast, little hard evidence has so far emerged of port facilities, or for exceptional groups of imported artefacts which could distinguish such sites from their neighbours as significant ports of entry. Was London pre-eminent, and, if so, was this because of the need to handle centrally all goods which were in, say, the hands of the procurator? Indeed,

9   M. Fulford, "The economy of Roman Britain," in M. Todd (ed.), *Recent research on Roman Britain* (Britannia Monograph 10, 1989) 175-201.

10   M. Fulford, "Roman London," *The London Journal* 20.2 (1995) 1-8.

11   B. J. Davies, B. Richardson and R. S. Tomber, *A dated corpus of Early Roman pottery from the City of London* (CBA Res. Rep. 98, 1995).

what was the scale of private as opposed to public commerce? Determining London's rôle as a port is of crucial importance for the history of Roman Britain. No more difficult in the resolution of this problem is the situation in the 4th c. On the one hand, there is the evidence, particularly from the first half of the 4th c., of considerable prosperity across the island; on the other, there is little evidence for an increased market from within Britain to account for it. If we assume that a good proportion of the perishables and raw materials from the villa and other estates was for export, who, apart from the imperial government, could have been a significant purchaser? Our evidence for ports around the coast is little stronger in the 4th c. than it was in the 2nd, but for London there is no certainty that an arrangement of wharves survived after the construction of the riverside section of the town wall (see Brigham above). Nevertheless, imports are documented from the late Roman town and the ceramic evidence shows a good representation of vessels from several, distant production sites in assemblages from the town.[12] Settlements along the roads leading into London show no evidence of decline before the second half of the 4th c. What happened to the traffic if it was not exported from London? The account of Julian's supply of corn to the Rhineland (Amm. Marc. 18.2.3) reveals centralised control; what better location to co-ordinate it from within Britain than London? Wharves or not, it is reasonable to argue continuity of the port function of the town to the end of the Roman administration.

In welcoming this review of recent archaeological work and *Interpreting London*, we should take the opportunity of developing from the feast before us a research agenda which tries to place London in a wider, provincial and imperial context, both in respect of its population and the way that it influenced the physical character of the city, and in respect of its functional rôle, principally as an entrepôt. At the same time there are many gaps in our knowledge of Roman London and Southwark, both spatially (what was, for example, the nature of the SW quarter of the town?) and chronologically. We need to know a great deal more about the late Roman town, as we do about Roman Southwark in all periods. Can a bridgehead settlement really have remained undefended? For all its unique qualities, London will continue to exert a particular fascination. The wealth of discoveries of the last 20 years reminds us that there is ample scope for new avenues for research.

---

12   R. P. Symonds and R. S. Tomber, "Late Roman London: an assessment of the ceramic evidence from the City of London," *TransLondMiddxArchSoc.* 62 (for 1991) [1994] 59-99; cf. P. Marsden, *Ships of the port of Roman London* (English Heritage Arch. Rep. 3, 1994) 105-8.